DAY WALKS OF NEW ZEALAND
Northland and Greater Auckland

Marios Gavalas has authored over 20 books on aspects of New Zealand's outdoors and history. He lives in Nelson, where he works as a tour guide.

Peter Janssen, a former publisher, has written many books on many subjects, outdoors, food, travel and pop culture among them. He lives in Auckland.

GW00808271

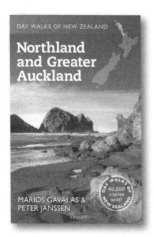

DAY WALKS OF NEW ZEALAND

Northland and Greater Auckland

MARIOS GAVALAS &
PETER JANSSEN

DAY WALKS OF NEW ZEALAND

Central Otago and Queenstown

PETER DYMOCK

DAY WALKS OF NEW ZEALAND

40,000 copies sold!

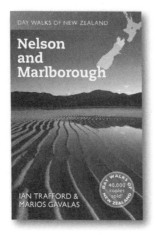

DAY WALKS OF NEW ZEALAND

Nelson and Marlborough

IAN TRAFFORD &
MARIOS GAVALAS

DAY WALKS OF NEW ZEALAND

Canterbury and Kaikoura

MARK PICKERING

DAY WALKS OF NEW ZEALAND

Northland and Greater Auckland

MARIOS GAVALAS & PETER JANSSEN

RAUPO

A RAUPO BOOK
Published by the Penguin Group
Penguin Group (NZ), 67 Apollo Drive, Rosedale,
Auckland 0632, New Zealand (a division of Pearson New Zealand Ltd)
Penguin Group (USA) Inc., 375 Hudson Street,
New York, New York 10014, USA
Penguin Group (Canada), 90 Eglinton Avenue East, Suite 700, Toronto,
Ontario, M4P 2Y3, Canada (a division of Pearson Penguin Canada Inc.)
Penguin Books Ltd, 80 Strand, London, WC2R 0RL, England
Penguin Ireland, 25 St Stephen's Green,
Dublin 2, Ireland (a division of Penguin Books Ltd)
Penguin Group (Australia), 250 Camberwell Road, Camberwell,
Victoria 3124, Australia (a division of Pearson Australia Group Pty Ltd)
Penguin Books India Pvt Ltd, 11, Community Centre,
Panchsheel Park, New Delhi – 110 017, India
Penguin Books (South Africa) (Pty) Ltd, 24 Sturdee Avenue,
Rosebank, Johannesburg 2196, South Africa

Penguin Books Ltd, Registered Offices: 80 Strand, London, WC2R 0RL, England

Day Walks of Northland first published by Reed Books, 2003
Day Walks of Greater Auckland first published by Reed Books, 2003

This combined edition first published by Penguin Group (NZ), 2011
1 3 5 7 9 10 8 6 4 2

Copyright © Marios Gavalas and Peter Janssen, 2003

The right of Marios Gavalas and Peter Janssen to be identified as the authors of this
work in terms of section 96 of the Copyright Act 1994 is hereby asserted.

Cover design by Anna Egan-Reid, © Penguin Group (NZ)
Printed in Australia by McPherson's Printing Group

ISBN 9780143567103

A catalogue record for this book is available
from the National Library of New Zealand.

www.penguin.co.nz

Contents

NORTHLAND

Preface   13

Acknowledgements   14

INTRODUCTION   16
  Geology   16
  Forest   18
  Native birds   20
  Pre-European history   23
  European arrival   24
  Kauri logging and gum digging   24
  Walking in Northland   25
    Safety   25
    Track grades   26
  New Zealand Environmental Care Code   27

WALKS ON AUPORI PENINSULA   28
Te Paki and Cape Reinga   28
  1 Cape Reinga Coastal Walkway   30
    Kapowairua to Pandora   30
    Pandora to Tapotupotu   31
    Tapotupotu to Cape Reinga   32
  2 Cape Reinga Lighthouse Walk   33
  3 Cape Reinga Coast Walk   34
  4 Te Werahi Gate to Te Werahi Beach   36
  5 Cape Reinga Road to Pandora   36

WALKS AROUND KAITAIA   38
  6 Kaitaia Walkway   38
  7 Herekino Forest Track   38

Karikari Peninsula   39
  8 Whangatupere Bay Walk   39
  9 Puheke Recreation Reserve Walk   40
 10 Gum Hole Reserve Walk   41
Omahuta Forest   42
 11 Omahuta Kauri Sanctuary Walk   43
 12 Kauri Stump Walk   43
Whangaroa   44
 13 Wairakau Stream Track   44
 14 Duke's Nose (Kairara Rocks)   45
 15 St Paul's Rock Summit Walk   46
 16 Mahinepua Peninsula Track   46

WALKS AROUND HOKIANGA AND DARGAVILLE   **48**
Hokianga Harbour   48
 17 Arai-te-uru Walk   48
Waipoua Forest   48
 18 Tane Mahuta   51
 19 Four Sisters Track   52
 20 Te Matua Ngahere   53
 21 Yakas Kauri Track   53
 22 Lookout Track   54
 23 Trounson Kauri Park   55
 24 Maunganui Bluff Walk   56
 25 Tokatoka Scenic Reserve Walk   57
 26 Kauri Bushmen's Memorial Walk   58

WALKS AROUND BAY OF ISLANDS AND WHANGARURU   **60**
Kerikeri   60
 27 Marsden Cross Historic Reserve Walk   60
 28 Kororipo Pa Walk   61
 29 Manginangina Kauri Walk   62
Paihia   63
 30 Haruru Falls Track/Waitangi National Trust
     Mangrove Walk   63

31 Opua Forest Lookout Track   65
32 Opua to Paihia Coastal Walkway   66

Russell   67
33 Toretore Island Walk   67
34 Flagstaff Hill   68
35 Motuarohia Island Track   69
36 Moturua Island Track   70
37 Urupukapuka Island Track   71
38 Cape Brett Track   72
39 Whangamumu Track   74
40 Kauri Grove Walk   75

Whangaruru   75
41 Ocean Beach Loop   75
42 Bland Bay Lookout Track   77
43 Mimiwhangata Coastal Park   78

Kawakawa   79
44 Ruapekapeka Pa Historic Reserve   79

WALKS AROUND WHANGAREI   **81**
45 Whananaki Coastal Walkway   81
46 Whale Bay to Matapouri Bay Loop Walk   82
47 Pukenui Forest Track   83
48 A.H. Reed Memorial Kauri Park   84
49 Whangarei Falls Scenic Reserve   85
50 Mt Manaia Track   86
51 Smugglers Bay Track   88
52 Peach Cove Track   89
53 Bream Head Track   90

Tangihua Forest   92
54 Kauri Dam Walk   92
55 Nature Walk   93

Waipu and Mangawhai   93
56 Waipu Caves Walkway   93
57 Brynderwyn Walkway   94
58 Mangawhai Cliffs Walkway   95

WALKS AROUND WARKWORTH   **97**
  59   Dome Forest Walkway   97
Tawharanui Regional Park   97
  60   Maori Bay Coast Walk/South Coast Loop Track   98
  61   North Coast Track   99
  62   Westend Track   99
Kawau Island   100
  63   Kawau Island Tracks   100
Other Warkworth walks   102
  64   Tamahunga Summit Trail   102
  65   Mt Auckland Walkway   102

MAPS
  1   Overview: Northland   15
  2   Far North   29
  3   Waipoua   50
  4   Bay of Islands   59

GREATER AUCKLAND

INTRODUCTION   **106**
  Top 12 walks   106
  Safety when walking in Greater Auckland   109
  Track grades   111
  New Zealand Environmental Care Code   112
  Birds of Greater Auckland   112

CITY WALKS   **118**
  1   Auckland Coast to Coast Walkway   119
  2   Cornwall Park/One Tree Hill/Maungakiekie   119
  3   Point England Walkway   120
  4   Tahuna Torea Nature Reserve   121
  5   Mangere Mountain   122
  6   Ambury Park   122
  7   Milford/Takapuna/Narrowneck Coastal Walk   123

8   North Head Historic Reserve Walk   124

9   Long Bay Regional Park Coastal Walk   126

SOUTHERN WALKS   **130**

10   Tawhitokino Bay Walk   131

11   Duder Regional Park   131

12   Tapapakanga Regional Park Coastal Walk   133

13   Waharau Ridge Loop Track   135

14   Mangatangi Trig   136

15   Hunua Falls/Cosseys Reservoir Walk   136

16   Wairoa Reservoir Walk, Hunua   139

17   Mount William Walkway   139

18   Awhitu Regional Park Farm Walk   140

WESTERN WALKS   **142**

19   Woodhill Forest Walk   144

20   Woodhill Forest Track/Rangitira Beach   144

21   Mokoroa Falls and Goldies Bush   145

22   Takapu Refuge Walk   146

23   Te Henga Coastal Walk (Bethells Beach)   150

24   Lake Wainamu Walkway   151

25   Cascade Kauri, Auckland City Walk, Waitakere Ranges Regional Park   152

26   Waitakere Dam Walk   153

27   Waitakere Tramline Walk (combine with the Waitakere Dam Walk)   153

28   Cascades Kauri Regional Park: Waitakere Dam Circuit   154

29   Fairy Falls Track   154

30   Fairy Falls/Old Coach Road Track   156

31   Anawhata Beach Track   156

32   Piha to Whites Beach   157

33   Lion Rock   158

34   Tasman Lookout Track   159

35   Kitekite Falls Walk (short)   160

36   Kitekite Falls Walk (long)   160

37 Mercer Bay Loop Walk 162
38 Te Ahuahu Road to Karekare Beach 162
39 Zion Hill Track to Karekare Beach Loop 163
40 Whatipu–Gibbons Track 165

NORTHERN WALKS **168**
41 Okura Bush Walkway 169
42 Wenderholm Regional Park Perimeter Track 170
43 Dome Forest Walkway 172
44 Mahurangi Regional Park: Cudlip Point Loop Track 173
45 Mahurangi Regional Park: Mita Bay Loop Track 173
46 Tamahunga Summit Trail 174
47 Goat Island Walkway 175
48 Tawharanui Regional Park: Maori Bay Coast Walk/
   South Coast Loop Track 178
49 Tawharanui Regional Park: North Coast Track 178
50 Tawharanui Regional Park: Westend Track 179
51 Mount Auckland Walkway 181

ISLANDS **182**
52 Great Barrier Island: Bridle Track 187
53 Great Barrier Island: DoC Office to Kaiarara Hut 187
54 Great Barrier Island: Kaiarara Hut to Mount Hobson
   via the Kaiarara Track 188
55 Great Barrier Island: Kaitoke Hot Springs 191
56 Great Barrier Island: Old Lady Track 192
57 Great Barrier Island: Palmers Track 193
58 Great Barrier Island: Warrens Track 194
59 Rangitoto Island Summit Track 194
60 Kawau Island Tracks 197
61 Tiritiri Matangi Island walks 199
62 Waiheke Island: Stoney Batter Walkway 203
63 Waiheke Island: Matiatia/Owhanake Loop 205

MAPS

1 (city walks 1–9, island walk 59)   117
2 (southern walks 10–17)   129
3a (western walks 19 and 20)   143
3b (western walks 21–30)   147
3c (western walks 31–40)   155
4 (northern walks 41–50, island walks 60 and 61)   167
5 (Great Barrier Island walks 52–58)   185

Northland

Preface

This guide is intended for the holidaymaker, local resident or tramper looking for a day walk in one of Northland's many areas of scenic splendour. The aim of this guide is to help you select the most rewarding walks from so many options.

For each walk, information on access to the start of the walk, notes on the state of the track and a short narrative on points of interest are provided.

Track grades are subjective and provided to help you choose a suitable walk. Please refer to the section on track grades (page 19) for an explanation of the system.

Approximate completion times are walking times and provided as a guide. They may vary according to the track conditions and your walking speed.

Some walks, especially around Te Paki, involve stream crossings and tidal sections. Make sure you are aware of tide times and consult the Department of Conversation (DoC) on stream levels before attempting these walks.

Other walks quote one-way times and may take a whole day. You should arrange appropriate transport to meet you at the other end or embark on the walk suitably prepared.

DoC has information centres in Whangarei, Bay of Islands and Waipoua Forest. It also runs offices in Kerikeri, Kaitaia and Te Paki.

Most walks described in this book are not suitable for dogs, as the walks traverse ecologically sensitive areas prone to disturbance.

The prevalence of thieves is an unfortunate nuisance, especially at quiet road ends. The surest way to deter them is to immobilise your vehicle and take all valuables with you.

If this guide enables you to visit somewhere you might not have otherwise discovered, or enhances your enjoyment of a morning walk along a deserted beach or in a lush green forest, then it has succeeded in its aim. Enjoy the walks!

Acknowledgements

Thanks to Keren who completed many of the walks with me and waited at the other end for those she didn't.

Our trusty 1971 VW Kombi, 'Betty', must be mentioned as she was our reliable vehicle and home for the duration of the research.

The meticulous notes of the Far North Regional Museum in Kaitaia and the help of the staff at Whangarei Library were invaluable.

At Reed, thanks to Peter Janssen for his support of the project and my editor Sam Hill.

A big thank you to all the DoC staff, without whose assistance the project could not have been completed. Their comments on the manuscript are much appreciated. In particular, thanks to Jon Maxwell, Lynell Greer, Katrina Upperton, Dene Harrison and Will Macrae. Darrell LimYock's ceaseless good humour on the trips to the islands was a source of inspiration.

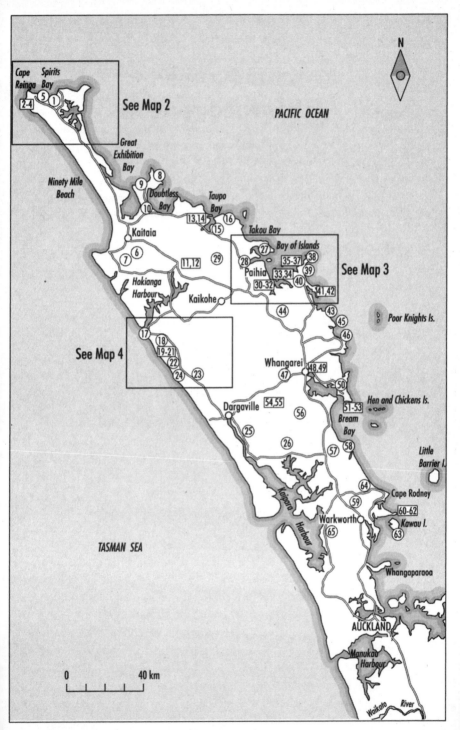

Northland walks

Introduction

The long finger of Northland stretches approximately 350 km from the Auckland isthmus to New Zealand's final accessible conclusion at Cape Reinga. Its snaking eastern coastline is studded with innumerable sandy bays and rocky headlands. On the west coast, an endless sandy sweep is punctuated only by the Hokianga and Kaipara harbours.

The rolling interior is a patchwork of farmland paddocks, with some extensive areas of mature forest, including the famous kauri giants of the Waipoua Forest.

A long history of human occupation, both Maori and Pakeha, has contributed to a colourful history, with many cultural artefacts to explore.

The region provides a magnificent mix of forest, coastal and historical walks, which explore this often remote, primeval and undiscovered landscape.

Geology

Northland's narrow finger of land stretches for around 350 km from the Auckland isthmus to Surville Cliffs near Cape Reinga. It has no mountain ranges, although there are some hills over 700 m around the Raetea and Waima forests. The rolling hill country and generally rounded relief is broken by many small rivers, inlets and harbours.

The extensive coastline, which is extremely long in relation to its area, exhibits marked contrasts between the coasts. The east coast shelters the drowned river valley harbours of Whangarei, Bay of Islands and Whangaroa, interspersed with a craggy intimate coastline of alternating rocky points and sandy beaches. Tranquil mangrove-filled backwaters form a necklace at the edge of the water.

The erosive powers of the sea have sculpted a sinuous labyrinth of bays, coves and inlets. Jagged headlands are constantly worked by waves to form offshore stacks, islets and reefs. The sumptuous sandy beaches nestled between the headlands are ripe for discovery, and many coastal walks such as the Whananaki Coastal Walkway, Opua to Paihia Coastal Walkway and Mimiwhangata Coastal Park allow unhurried exploration.

On the west coast, the relentless currents of the Tasman Sea have smoothed a shore of even contour and a seemingly endless windswept stretch of sand, almost unbroken from Kaipara to Ninety Mile Beach. The uniformity of the coast is punctuated by the extensive harbours of Hokianga and Kaipara. Both have treacherous sandbars and reach significantly inland. No part of Northland is more than 40 km from the sea.

Te Paki is an anomaly, isolated at the tip of the long, sandy Aupori Peninsula. Sand, derived form the central North Island volcanoes, has been transported to the coast and slowly blown to form the sandy appendage. The former island archipelago, which was separated by a shallow sea, is now joined to the mainland. The Cape Reinga Coast Walk discovers some of the other-worldliness of the most massive dune systems in the country.

Northland breaks the standard New Zealand mould of a country being twisted and squeezed by tectonic forces. During the long period of immobility, the landscape has been smoothed to its present subdued contours. A warm, moist climate has deeply weathered the exposed mantle of rock.

Most rocks are either sedimentary or volcanic. Sedimentary rocks usually formed in shallow marine basins, to be later compacted, heated and thrust up to re-emerge. Shells and skeletal remains of marine creatures have formed limestone.

Forested headlands collared with a frothing ring of white water are conspicuous around the Northland coast.

Volcanoes have sprung cones and the lava debris poured out have contributed to some of the most spectacular formations such as Bream Head, Mt Manaia and the Tangihua Range. The agents of erosion — sun, wind, rain, time, rivers and waves — have since remodelled the landforms to the shapes seen today.

The subtropical latitude, warm, wet climate and proximity to the sea mean summers can be humid and winter can be characterised by a high rainfall. This can fall with intensity in northeasterly winds. Northland's mean annual rainfall is 1000–1300 mm, rising to 2500 mm in the ranges. The subtropical high-pressure belt causes a third of precipitation to fall in winter and a fifth in summer. Frosts are rare and light, hence the term 'winterless north'.

Forest

Northland was once a sea of green. Maori left much of the forest alone, believing it to be the realm of Tane, God of the Forest. Originally Northland was cloaked in a dense broadleaf podocarp rainforest with kauri the dominant forest type in areas of strong relief.

Kauri (*Agathis australis*) is the most renowned species among indigenous forest types. It had an irregular distribution, but formed isolated pure stands. It was often found in small stands on shallow ridge soils and spurs. It now occurs in mixed forest with podocarp and sometimes hardwoods.

Waipoua Forest contains the largest remaining kauri stands and the largest trees, many of which retain their Maori names. Tane Mahuta and Te Matua Ngahere are some of Northland's biggest tourist drawcards, and rightly so. Their unparalleled majesty and monumental presence is a pitiful reminder of what once was.

No other forest type played a more significant role in the economy of

The kauri is the most famous tree of Northland and New Zealand, and used to dominate the forest.

early New Zealand. From initial discovery in 1772 to the decline of the industry due to depletion in the early 1900s, logging, and the associated gum digging, contributed to the nation's wealth. Only remoteness and inaccessibility saved many trees, such as those in the Omahuta Kauri Sanctuary, from axe and saw. By 1975 the total area of mature kauri forest in Northland was reduced to 6240 ha, less than 1 percent of the original cover.

The kauri forest develops a unique character with strong associations, some noted by botanist Leonard Cockayne in the early 1900s. Dense swards of *Astelia trinervia* (kauri grass) and tussocks of *Gahnia xanthocarpa*, a giant cutting sedge, often predominate beneath the huge trees.

Podocarps inhabit high ground, with totara and miro the dominant species, but locally heavy stands of rimu occur. Kahikatea predominates on areas with poor drainage.

Broadleaf forest is most represented in Northland because it can rapidly regenerate. Tawa, towai and tawari grow at higher altitudes, while taraire and associated kohekohe predominate on lower slopes and in the valleys.

A mixed podocarp-broadleaf forest is widely distributed with a usually dense broadleaf understorey of taraire, tawa, mahoe and wineberry.

Manuka and kanuka act as nursery species, forming a dense canopy that shelters vulnerable seedlings. Areas where they are present indicate the land may have been dug over repeatedly for gum or been returned from pasture.

On the coast, karaka, kawakawa and pohutukawa are common. Low-lying areas are smothered in manuka, flax and cabbage trees. The waterlogged gumland soils have manuka, bracken fern and rushes.

The coastal fringe is bordered by extensive mangrove forests, which grow to be significant trees in the warm and humid climate of Northland. Mangroves (*Avicennia marina* ssp. *australasica*) bind the muds of the estuarine edges and form a diverse and bountiful ecosystem, which supports crustaceans, molluscs, fish and bird species. The mangroves also prevent erosion of vulnerable shorelines.

Northland was the first region in New Zealand to be settled and was therefore the cradle of European farming. Forest cover was removed for logging and fires raged to clear the land for agriculture. Only 13 percent of indigenous forest remains. Isolated podocarps occur as individual trees or small stands on the now extensive mosaic of farmland paddocks.

The introduction of goats, deer and pigs, which browse the accessible foliage, has severely reduced the health and diversity of the forest understorey. Possums, which find many of the defenceless New Zealand species such as rata and mamaku palatable, have left skeletons where once there were vigorous trees.

Waipoua was the birthplace of a conservation movement, when the Waipoua Preservation Society attracted nationwide support in 1952. Some 9105 ha were set aside when the Waipoua Forest Sanctuary was established.

The Department of Conservation is entrusted with the massive task of managing the remaining forests. Predator control programmes such as those at Trounson Kauri Park are meeting with some success. The health and diversity of the forest is enhanced, with a commensurate improvement in bird populations.

Native birds

The songs of native birds can be conspicuously absent from the Northland forest. An eerie quietness often presides over the forest interior. Introduced predators and habitat clearance have kept bird populations low and the forest devoid of its most tuneful residents.

Occasionally your attention may be caught by the sudden appearance of a fantail, perched on a nearby branch. The whistling sound of a kereru's wings may cause your attention to turn skywards. Perhaps the dulcet calls of a tui or bellbird may even cause you to stop and search the canopy in an attempt to catch a glimpse of the musical genius.

These encounters occur with unfortunate rarity. Human arrival meant the introduction of mammalian predators, at first rats and dogs with

Nurtured by a mild climate and abundant rainfall, the Northland forest is a luxuriant mix of species, tropical in its diversity and character.

Maori and later, with Europeans, rats, cats and mustelids. The rats, mice and feral cats climb trunks and negotiate the branches to feed on eggs and chicks. Stoats, ferrets and weasels are attracted to nestlings, and prey on the defenceless chicks while the parents are away feeding.

Vast tracts of forest have been cleared for agricultural purposes. The diminished habitat has resulted in declining populations of many New Zealand birds including the kiwi, kaka and kokako.

On the coast, the habitat and breeding areas of terns, oystercatchers and dotterels have been decimated by building and competitive land uses. Shallow, exposed nests fall prey to feral cats, domestic dogs and vehicles. Some species such as the New Zealand dotterel are now very rare.

Predator control programmes implemented by DoC are aimed at reversing this decline and are meeting with some success. The fencing off of coastal breeding grounds and increasing public awareness are allowing populations to recover. Where warning signs are posted, heed their advice and keep away, especially during the spring and summer breeding seasons.

These are some forest residents you will meet:

Fantail/Piwakawaka (*Rhipidura fuliginosa*)

The friendly fantail will greet you with an energetic 'cheep' as you pause to rest. Performing aerial acrobatics between perches and displaying its livery on alighting, the fantail will always succeed in attracting your attention. Fantails will often follow you, preying on the insects disturbed as you pass.

The fantail feeds from dawn to dusk, executing skilful movements in mid-air to catch flying insects. Males will show off to visitors by dropping their wings and fanning their tails.

Bellbird/Korimako (*Anthornis melanura*)

The bellbird is often heard, but rarely seen, as its sweet song is carried through the vegetation. These bell-like notes are learned from neighbouring adults of the same sex or parents.

Often bellbirds are heard in tandem, singing and counter-singing to determine territorial spacing. Pairs are monogamous and may duet.

These honeyeaters take nectar from many native trees. In autumn, by feeding on berries, they act as important seed-dispersing agents in the ecology of the forest.

Tui/Parson bird (*Prosthemadera novaeseelandiae*)

The melodic tones of the tui often penetrate the forest interior. Singing from dawn to dusk, the tui resonates a formidable repertoire of pure bell-like notes. These virtuoso musicians can compose a symphonic range of songs. Distinguished by aristocratic white throat feathers, the tui is an important member of the forest community. By eating nectar and fruit and often travelling large distances to abundant food sources, the tui helps disperse seeds and pollinates plants.

New Zealand pigeon/Kereru (*Hemiphaga novaeseelandiae*)

The herbivorous pigeon will be seen either feeding voraciously on a variety of native fruits or resting on a sunny perch digesting its meal. It will give itself away by causing berries to drop from the canopy while gorging on a feast of fruit.

Its preferred diet is composed of the larger-fruited podocarps such as miro and matai. Species such as tawa, taraire and karaka rely heavily on the kereru for the dispersal of their seeds.

Because of its wide gape, the kereru can eat large fruit. Little abrasion of the seed occurs in the gizzard, allowing seeds to pass through the digestive system intact. In this way the kereru ensures the perpetuation of its food source.

On the coast look for these birds:

New Zealand dotterel (*Charadrius obscurus*)

The shy and reserved cheeps of the threatened New Zealand dotterel accompany a walk along many Northland beaches. Pairs are loyal and usually within sight of each other. They step lightly like ballerinas over the sand and keep a safe distance from humans. They may fake a broken wing to discourage you from passing too close to nests.

They lay camouflaged eggs in shallow hollows in the dunes and their nests are prone to disturbance. Keep dogs under control and keep out of fenced areas during the breeding season.

Variable oystercatcher (*Haematopus unicolor*)

These endemic birds vary from pied to black in colour, and are larger than the (always pied and cosmopolitan) South Island pied oystercatcher. They are normally seen in pairs and kick up a vociferous racket when approached. Their whistling cheeps are projected at the slightest chance of intrusion and they will often walk a considerable distance up the beach before taking flight.

They fly low to the water with a powerful wing flap and feed on sandy beaches and spits, and in harbours and estuaries. They probe shallow water, sand and mud to extract marine worms, molluscs and larger bivalve shells. Often their footprints can be traced to encircle a bivalve, whose shells they prise open with their long red bills.

Caspian tern (*Hydroprogne caspia*)

Distinguished from the more boisterous red-billed gull by pointed wings and a more erratic wing flap, the Caspian tern is an expert diver.

Deftly spying fish by hovering above the water, they can dive with expert aerobatic skills to capture their prey.

Their red bill and black 'cap' contrast with their white bodies and grey wings. They will often be seen in flocks resting on offshore stacks or coastal rocky outcrops.

Pre-European history

According to Maori mythology, the legendary Maui is said to have fished up the North Island (Te Ika a Maui), which is likened to a stingray (whai). The head is located around Wellington and its tail protrudes north. In this representation, Northland is the Te Hiku o te Ika, the tail of the fish.

Northland has a long history of Maori occupation. The great explorer Kupe is said to have landed at Hokianga, leaving two taniwha to guard the treacherous harbour entrance. Many descendants of the migratory canoes, which voyaged from eastern Polynesia, settled in Northland and developed their cultures.

Maori populations were densely distributed and mainly concentrated in pa on the headlands. These fortified sites were often defended with ditches and palisades. Cultivation of kumara and taro took place on nearby terraces, many of which are still evident today. Headlands such as Tawharanui, high hills such as Maunganui Bluff, and natural fortresses such as Ruapekapeka pa are replete with stories, history and legend.

Some walks such as Kororipo pa and Urupukapuka Island Track help give you an idea of their way of life, and interpretation panels bring to life the well-preserved evidence. Middens have been scoured by archaeologists to determine early inhabitants' diets, mainly based on the bountiful resources of the sea.

Many of the legendary explorers such as Tohe, who journeyed along Ninety Mile Beach (Te-Oneroa-a-Tohe), left a legacy in the naming of landmarks.

Cape Reinga (Te Rerengawairua) is the departing point for spirits on their journey to the underworld. The walks around Te Paki take in some of the area's rich cultural history.

European arrival

In 1769, Captain James Cook aboard the *Endeavour* sailed north up Northland's east coast. In late November, he found what he described as a 'noble anchorage' between Moturua and Motuarohia islands in the Bay of Islands. Despite a few skirmishes, Cook was able to observe the Maori way of life and trade with inhabitants. He rounded Cape Reinga and described what he saw as the 'Desart Coast'.

Marion du Fresne's French expedition in 1772 met with less welcoming intentions. With a crew weary from scurvy and ships in need of repair, they set up camp on Moturua Island. After initial friendly exchanges, relations deteriorated, with many of the crew later being slaughtered and eaten.

A sorry fate also met the passengers of the *Boyd* in Whangaroa Harbour in 1809, with the ship accidentally being set alight after a hostile attack.

It was with this intimidating legacy that the first missionaries arrived. Samuel Marsden preached the first Christian sermon in New Zealand on Christmas Day 1814 at Oihi Bay on the Purerua Peninsula in the Bay of Islands. He set up a mission station and under the guard of Hongi Hika expanded his activities to Kerikeri.

In 1840 the Treaty of Waitangi, an agreement between Maori chiefs and the British that set out the degree of sovereignty the British had over the new colony, was signed. Later disputes resulted in the flagpole of Flagstaff Hill being cut down by Hone Heke and the Battle of the North, which culminated at Ruapekapeka pa.

Kauri logging and gum digging

The growth of the new colony prompted exploitation of Northland's natural resources, mainly kauri timber. The forest giants were mercilessly felled from around the 1850s onwards in an almost complete annihilation of the majestic trees. The Kauri Stump Walk in the Omahuta Forest gives a good impression of the size of the trees felled. The timber was used for boat building, house building and furniture making. Some of the trees they left are thankfully still standing in the Waipoua Forest and Omahuta Kauri Sanctuary.

The extraction involved a high degree of human endeavour, with tramlines, bush railways, driving dams and bush tracks being constructed to remove the massive logs from the rugged watersheds to the coastal mills. Little evidence of the infrastructure remains today.

The associated gum digging industry was concentrated around the northern reaches of Northland and the Aupori Peninsula. Lumps of matured gum, preserved in swamps over millennia, were excavated in primitive condition for use in the manufacture of varnish. Only scant accessible evidence of the pits dug to probe the ground remains on the Karikari Peninsula.

Walking in Northland

Safety

- Always check the weather forecast before departing. Weather can change very quickly.
- It can rain with unabated ferocity any time of the year in Northland. If it has been raining previous to or during your walk, streams may be at flood level. Do not attempt to cross a stream in flood. Wait until it subsides.
- Some walks involve crossing streams and rivers. Make sure the water level is safe to cross and check tide times for tidal walks along the coast.
- Always take enough water, food and, if necessary, shelter for your walk. Make sure you are fit enough for the grade of walk you are attempting.
- Possum trappers use many tracks through the forest. They mark their routes with *pink* triangles. Do not follow these. Follow *orange* triangles only. Other common track markers include orange rectangles, which look like pieces of Venetian blinds, and orange posts lining a route. Take care as sometimes markers can be sporadic. If you are in any doubt return to your last known point and proceed from there.
- Inform a friend, relative or DoC Visitor Centre of your intended itinerary before departing on walks into rugged backcountry.

- Take a detailed map and compass. These will not only aid navigation but also inform you of interesting features in the area.
- Many walks pass through concealed valleys and remote coastal areas. Cellphone repeater stations are scarce. Do not rely on cellphones as safety devices, even on the summits of hills.

Track grades

Please note that these grades are subjective and provided as a guide only. Tracks are graded according to length, gradient and surface.

Grade 1: Track surface is metalled or even with only minor undulations. Directions are clearly signposted. Walks usually take less than half an hour.

Grade 2: Track may be metalled or unmetalled. It is clearly marked and well formed but usually involves some inclines.

Grade 3: Track is unmetalled but well formed and usually marked. Can be uneven and boggy with frequent inclines.

Grade 4: Track is usually formed but may be marked or unmarked. It may be very steep, uneven or boggy. Walks of this grade are more appropriate for people of good fitness with some outdoor experience.

For walks graded 2 and above, you should be adequately prepared with supplies of food and water. It is advisable to wear strong shoes, preferably sturdy boots, and take a detailed map (for example a 1:50,000 Topomap).

Where a track can be attempted from both directions, the descriptions given in the book apply to one direction only. If you attempt a walk in one direction only, make sure you arrange suitable transport to meet you at the walk's conclusion.

Marked tracks usually have orange triangles or rectangles nailed to trees. Each marker is usually visible from the previous one, but marking can sometimes be sporadic. If you think you have strayed from the track, retrace your steps to the last reference marker. Do not follow pink, blue or yellow triangles. They are there to guide possum trappers and managers of bait stations and drop lines.

New Zealand Environmental Care Code

When walking in Northland, follow the Environmental Care Code.
- Protect rare and endangered plants and animals.
- Remove rubbish. Take it away with you.
- Bury toilet waste in a shallow hole away from waterways, tracks, campsites and huts.
- Keep streams clean.
- Take care with fires. If you must build a fire, keep it small, use dead wood, and douse it with water when you leave. Before you go, remove any evidence. Portable stoves are preferable, as they are more efficient and pose less risk to the environment.
- After camping, leave the site as you found it.
- Keep to the track. This minimises the chances of treading on fragile seedlings.
- Respect the cultural heritage.
- Enjoy yourself.
- Consider others. Respect everybody's reasons for wanting to enjoy Northland's beauty.

Some walks are made easier as they have boardwalks, steps or walkways.

Walks on Aupori Peninsula

Te Paki and Cape Reinga

Around five million years ago, the Aupori Peninsula, including Te Paki, was a series of islets, an archipelago separated by shallow seas. With the onset and waning of ice ages, sea levels fluctuated and large sandspits formed, sculpted by the prevailing southwesterly winds. Te Paki thus became joined to the greater North Island landmass, but still retains an island character. It feels like a different land.

To Maori the area around Cape Reinga is sacred. After journeying up Ninety Mile Beach, a spirit will climb a high hill called Haumu and bid farewell to the land of the living. It drinks from the stream called Te-wai-o-ngunguru ('Waters of the Underworld') and travels down the exposed root of the legendary pohutukawa at Cape Reinga. From there it travels to the Manawa-Tahi (Three Kings Islands), meaning 'last breath', and on to the mythical homeland of Hawaiki.

Te Paki station originally covered over 100,000 acres (over 40,000 ha) and was acquired by Samuel Yates. He owned 8000 sheep and 2000 cattle, and employed over 300 diggers to search for gum. Cattle from the station were usually driven down Ninety Mile Beach and his wool was shipped from Tapotupotu Bay. He married a local chief's daughter and was known as 'King of the North' until his death in 1900.

Richard Keene, a Wellington businessman, then bought Te Paki Station, and his family sold the 42,176 acres (over 17,000 ha) to the government in 1966. They leased the land to a company who tried in vain to grow tung trees to manufacture tung oil. The venture was thwarted because of the lack of shelter, but a few examples still grow in the valleys.

The area around Te Paki and North Cape is an outstanding habitat for rare and unique species of flora and fauna. The geographical isolation has led to subspecies evolving differently from their mainland counterparts.

The track network around Te Paki is extensive, especially along the spectacular coastline. It is possible to walk from Kapowairua to Cape Reinga via the Cape Reinga Coastal Walkway, then continue to Te Paki Stream along Ninety Mile Beach via the Cape Reinga Coast Walk.

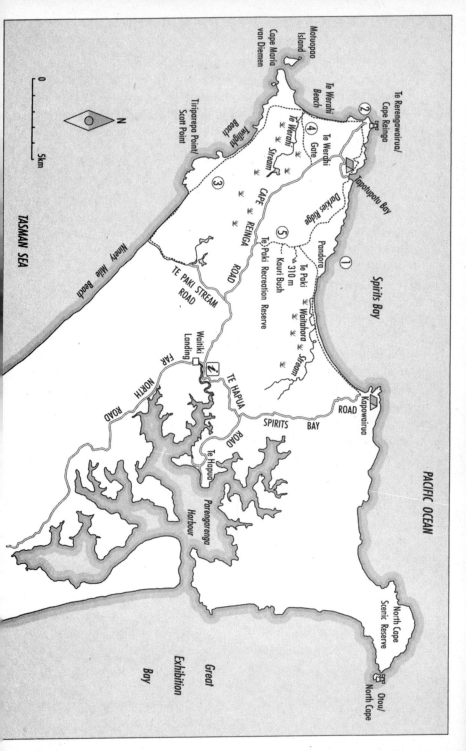

Far North

These day walks can be broken into stages and you will need to arrange suitable transport to meet you at the other end.

Tracks at Te Paki often cross beaches and meander along small bays. At the ends of the bays are orange rectangles on posts, indicating where to rejoin the track. These are usually easy to find, but in some instances they have succumbed to erosion or take a little searching to locate.

Some of the tracks involve stream crossings. The Waitahora Stream at the western end of Spirits Bay is a deep crossing and should be attempted only at low tide, as should the creek on the eastern side of Tapotupotu Bay. Te Werahi Creek at the southern end of Te Werahi Beach can be crossed at mid–low tide. Seek advice from DoC in Kaitaia or Te Paki before embarking on these walks.

From the end of State Highway (SH) 1F at Waitiki Landing the roads become unsealed. They are narrow and winding and carry a large volume of traffic on the pilgrimage north to Cape Reinga.

The wetlands at the foot of the hills harbour breeding grounds for mosquitoes, which swarm in large numbers, especially in summer. By day, when the mosquitoes are asleep, the sandflies come on shift. Bring insect repellent in large quantities.

DoC has campgrounds at Kapowairua (open only in summer) and Tapotupotu Bay. These have toilets and water and at Tapotupotu Bay there are also cold-water showers. Toilets are situated at Cape Reinga and Te Paki Stream carpark.

1 Cape Reinga Coastal Walkway

Kapowairua to Pandora

GRADE 2

TIME 2½ hours one way along beach; 2 hours one way behind dunes; 4½ hours return

ACCESS Kapowairua is at the end of Spirits Bay Road. Follow signs to Spirits Bay along Te Hapua Road, 21 km before Cape Reinga. After 6 km turn left into Spirits Bay Road.

The track behind the dunes is signposted on the left just before the road ends.

TRACK NOTES

• The sand on the beach is soft, making progress arduous.

- Behind the dunes, follow orange marker posts along the vehicle track, which remains even.
- To reach Pandora requires a crossing of the Waitahora Stream. This can be made only at low tide. The stream is deep and may involve getting wet to your waist. Check with DoC on stream levels before attempting the walk.

POINTS OF INTEREST

- A 9 lb cannon on the hill above the parking area at the campground was owned by Hongi Keepa, who acquired it from a whaler in the early 1800s. A plaque beneath describes its convoluted history.
- The vast wetland behind the dunes harbours thriving communities of bitterns, rails, paradise ducks and mosquitoes.
- The great chief of the Aupori tribe, Tohe, dreamed his daughter, who lived beyond Hokianga, was ill and resolved to visit her. He journeyed down Ninety Mile Beach, naming landmarks along the way. He vowed his spirit would return if he failed in the completion of his dangerous journey. News of his death was relayed by the servant who accompanied him and the promise of his return was fulfilled by his spirit. Spirits Bay thus received its name and is also referred to as Piwhane Bay.
- A large number of human bones have been unearthed around Spirits Bay, suggesting the area may have been a battleground or burial site.
- When Captain Cook passed in 1769, he noted a village on the western hills overlooking the bay. Evidence of terraces and hangi pits are still visible from near the Waitahora Stream.
- In 1772, Marion du Fresne and his French expedition anchored off Spirits Bay and sent parties ashore for water. One ship lost two anchors in a severe storm.

Pandora to Tapotupotu

GRADE 4

TIME 3½ hours one way

ACCESS Tapotupotu Bay is reached by turning right onto Tapotupotu Road, 2.5 km before Cape Reinga. It is 3 km along the winding unsealed road to the bay.

The track at Tapotupotu is signposted from the far side of the Tapotupotu Stream opposite the most easterly point of the campground.

Pandora can be reached only by walking the length of Spirits Bay and crossing the Waitahora Stream.

TRACK NOTES

- At low tide from Pandora you can skirt the base of the headlands by walking over the rocks. Otherwise a high-tide route is signposted and marked with orange posts over the two headlands. The long grass has a worn track through it, but can be steep and muddy (45 minutes).
- The track then climbs steadily along a vehicle track for 45 minutes to a signposted junction with Darkies Ridge.
- From here it is 2 hours to reach Tapotupotu along an old vehicle track and grass track lined with orange posts. The track heads to a cliff-top ridge and descends steeply to Tapotupotu Bay.

POINTS OF INTEREST

- The camp that occupied the grass clearing at Pandora was run by Captain Hector McQuarrie in the 1920s. The bush huts were made from local materials and there were colourful canvas roofs. The wreck of the steamer *Kahu* provided timber for the 'excellent floor' of the dancehall and the salvaged sail gave shelter.
- The camp was advertised as being 'Away up where New Zealand Ends' and was frequented by the well heeled of the 'carriage trade' needing an escape. It was an arduous journey up Ninety Mile Beach and over the steep hills to the camp, but rewarded with scenic beauty and solitude.
- Pandora is named after HMS *Pandora*, a survey ship that visited the coast in 1849.

Tapotupotu to Cape Reinga

GRADE 3

TIME 1½ hours one way

ACCESS Tapotupotu Bay is reached by turning right onto Tapotupotu Road, 2.5 km before Cape Reinga. It is 3 km along the winding unsealed road to the bay.

The track starts from the orange rectangle on a post at the western side of the bay. The track exits above the eastern side of the carpark at Cape Reinga.

TRACK NOTES

- The track is marked with orange posts.
- For 20 minutes follow the track through grass to the ridge, where it enters low scrub (20 minutes). The 20-minute descent to Sandy Bay is steep, from where it is a 30-minute steady climb to Cape Reinga.

- In places the track hovers on the cliff top. Beware of strong wind gusts.

POINTS OF INTEREST

- The dramatic sheer cliffs, sandy beaches of Tapotupotu, Sandy Bay and the views from Cape Reinga to North Cape are highlights of this walk.

2 Cape Reinga Lighthouse Walk

GRADE 1

TIME 20 minutes return

ACCESS The start of the track is signposted from the carpark at the end of Cape Reinga Road. There are toilets nearby.

TRACK NOTES The sealed track is wide and even, descending to the lighthouse above Cape Reinga.

POINTS OF INTEREST

- The concrete tower of Cape Reinga lighthouse is 10 m tall and stands 165 m above sea level. The lens was shipped from England and installed on Motuopao Island in 1879. Cape Reinga lighthouse started operating in 1941.
- According to Maori mythology, the final leg of a spirit's journey involves travelling down the exposed root of the legendary pohutukawa at Te Rerengawairua ('The spirits that leap' — Cape Reinga). From there it travels to the Manawa-Tahi (Three Kings Islands), and on to Hawaiki.
- The pohutukawa tree is named Akakite-reinga and is just visible between the two prominent humps that form the cape.
- The frothing water to the west is Columbia Bank, a swirling maelstrom of confused water, where the calm female waters of the Pacific Ocean meet the furious disturbed waters of the male Tasman Sea. The upwelling of nutrients attracts abundant fish and marine life.
- Cape Reinga is 3 km south of Surville Cliffs, which are 1 km north of North Cape. The cape is the most northerly accessible point on the New Zealand mainland. A steady stream of tour buses and visitors, both domestic and from overseas, make the pilgrimage to this wondrous and awe-inspiring place.
- To the north, the Three Kings Islands were named on the eve of Epiphany by Abel Tasman, to commemorate the Three Wise Men of the East, who followed the star to Bethlehem.

3 Cape Reinga Coast Walk

GRADE 4

TIME 7 hours one way; 8½ hours one way including detour to Cape Maria van Diemen; 1¼ hours to southern end of Te Werahi Beach

ACCESS The start of the track is signposted to Te Werahi Beach from the carpark at Cape Reinga. Alternatively you can start the walk from Te Paki Stream carpark, which is 4 km down Te Paki Stream Road, 17 km before Cape Reinga.

You can also join the walk via Te Werahi Gate to Te Werahi Beach track.

TRACK NOTES

- From Cape Reinga (Te Rerengawairua) the wide track weaves for 30 minutes down to Te Werahi Beach, which takes 45 minutes to traverse along firm sand.
- The track to Te Werahi Gate departs from the southern end of the beach and is indicated with an orange rectangle on a post (see Te Werahi Gate to Te Werahi Beach track description, number 4 on page 29).
- At the southern end of Te Werahi Beach is Te Werahi Stream, which should preferably be crossed at low tide but can be crossed at mid tide.
- Large orange triangles on posts indicate the track over the Herangi Hill dunes to the signposted Cape Maria van Diemen turnoff (45 minutes). This 1½-hour detour drops down the southern side of a large sand bowl for 20 minutes before climbing a steep grass bank along a formed but unmarked track to the light station (25 minutes). Return to the main track by the same route.
- It's a further 45 minutes along an old vehicle track through low vegetation to the northwestern end of Twilight Beach (Te Paengarehia). Twilight Beach takes 40 minutes to walk.
- At the southeastern end an old vehicle track crosses Scotts Point for 1½ hours through low vegetation. Take care following the orange marker posts as there is a network of tracks excavated through the mantle of thin peat soils to the bedrock below. Tracks are wide and firm.
- The final 10 minutes over Scotts Point to Kahokawa Beach, at the northernmost tip of Ninety Mile Beach, drops via wooden steps.
- It takes around 1 hour to walk Ninety Mile Beach along firm sand to reach Te Paki Stream (Kauaeparaoa Stream), from where it is a further 1 hour to reach the carpark. You will have to walk along the bed of the shallow sandy stream.

- Beware of vehicles on Ninety Mile Beach and Te Paki Stream, which is the main northern access point for vehicles using the beach.

POINTS OF INTEREST
- The vast dune systems evident around Cape Maria van Diemen and Te Paki Stream are the product of sand accretion. Sediment transported to the coast by the rivers from the central North Island volcanoes has been blown up the coast by the prevailing winds. It has accumulated to form the dunes, some over 150 m high, which are awash with vibrant and varied colours.
- The dunes around Herangi Hill at the base of Cape Maria van Diemen are a colourful composition of reds, ochres, peach, white and golden sands. The mantle of caked sand is mottled with rock, shells of the flax snail and tufts of orange pingao.
- The almost extinct land snail *Placostylus ambagiosus* is prevalent in the area, but populations have been ravaged by wild pigs. Fossilised shells have been found in the dunes near Cape Maria van Diemen. The species occurs only in the Solomon Islands and Fiji, suggesting the connection of these landmasses by land bridges to New Zealand in times of lower sea level.
- Cape Maria van Diemen was named by Abel Tasman on 5 January 1643 to honour the wife of the Governor of Batavia.
- Twilight Beach was named after the wreck of the schooner *Twilight*, which sunk on 25 March 1871, with the loss of two lives. In 1966 the collier *Kaitawa* also sunk nearby. All 29 crew members drowned. Wreckage from the wheelhouse was later retrieved from the beach. The beach was formerly known as Rahu Bay.
- To Maori, Ninety Mile Beach is known as Te-Oneroa-a-Tohe, meaning 'The long beach of Tohe'. According to Maori mythology, a spirit will travel north with a token of its home in hand. This will be deposited at Te Arai in the form of twigs, seaweed or a sprig of leaves. The spirit then climbs a high hill called Haumu and bids farewell to the land of the living, before travelling down the exposed root of the legendary pohutukawa at Cape Reinga. From there it travels to the Three Kings Islands and the mythical Hawaiki.
- The source of the name of Ninety Mile Beach is a mystery; however, one theory refers to Scotts Point. It is named after an early European settler, who grazed sheep near present-day Ahipara, at the southern end of the beach. In autumn, he would drive them up the beach to Scotts Point to graze. As he was the only Pakeha in those days to travel

the beach, he was often asked of its length. His response of 'Ninety Miles' became commonly used and the misnomer has stuck.

- From the southern side of Scotts Point there are quintessential views of Ninety Mile Beach. The beach is masked by a haze of spray in the far distance, while the rolling crests of folding waves retreat to the horizon. Matapia Island stands out to sea.

4 Te Werahi Gate to Te Werahi Beach

GRADE 3

TIME 2 hours return

ACCESS Te Werahi Gate is signposted on the left, 4.5 km before Cape Reinga.

TRACK NOTES

- The track is well formed and marked with large orange triangles on posts. Orange rectangles on posts lead over the dunes near the beach.
- The track crosses paddocks for 15 minutes before crossing a stile and descending the hill to a boardwalk (15 minutes).
- Climb the small hill through manuka scrub for 15 minutes to the dunes, which exit at the southern end of beach.

POINTS OF INTEREST

- Te Werahi Beach is an open stretch of golden sand, bordered by dunes and hills. Cape Maria van Diemen marks its southern side and was named by Abel Tasman when he sailed past in 1643.
- This walk makes a worthwhile excursion for those not wanting to attempt the longer walks in the region.

5 Cape Reinga Road to Pandora

GRADE 3

TIME 3 hours return; add 1 hour if including detour to Kauri Bush; add 45 minutes if including detour to Te Paki Trig

ACCESS The Pandora track is signposted 11.5 km before Cape Reinga and 4.5 km after Te Paki Stream Road.

TRACK NOTES

- The walk follows an old vehicle track through low manuka scrub. After 30 minutes a detour to Kauri Bush is signposted on the right.

- This 1 hour-return walk becomes steeper, narrower and more overgrown as it descends to the stream. Return via the same track.
- After 15 minutes another detour to Te Paki summit is signposted on the right. The return to the trig takes 45 minutes.
- The junction with Darkies Ridge is a further 5 minutes. From here, it is 2 hours to Tapotupotu Bay and a 45-minute descent to Pandora.

POINTS OF INTEREST

- Some sizeable kauri give a scant impression of the forest that once cloaked the area around Te Paki. The reason for the forest's disappearance is not known, although some land was cleared for farming.
- The best views to Spirits Bay (Piwhane Bay) and North Cape are from the ridge to Te Paki summit (310 m). At the trig the vegetation obscures the views.
- The camp that occupied the grass clearing at Pandora was run by Captain Hector McQuarrie in the 1920s. The bush huts were made from local materials and there were colourful canvas roofs. The wreck of the steamer *Kahu* provided timber for the 'excellent floor' of the dancehall and the salvaged sail gave shelter.
- The camp was advertised as being 'Away up where New Zealand Ends' and was frequented by the well heeled of the 'carriage trade' needing an escape. It was an arduous journey up Ninety Mile Beach and over the steep hills to the camp, but rewarded with scenic beauty and solitude.
- Pandora is named after HMS *Pandora*, a survey ship that visited the coast in 1849.

Walks around Kaitaia

6 Kaitaia Walkway

GRADE 3

TIME 2¼ hours return

ACCESS From Kaitaia, follow SH 1 for 3 km and turn right into Larmer Road. Continue 3 km to the junction with the quarry. Bear right along the unsealed road and continue 2 km to the road end, where there is a small parking bay. The start of the track is signposted.

TRACK NOTES

- The track is marked with orange triangles.
- For 20 minutes it is wide and metalled, then crosses a stream. You have to head upstream a few metres and may get wet feet. The track standard then deteriorates, becoming narrower and muddy, with slippery planks over some hazards.
- After 30 minutes you come to a junction: left is a 20-minute-return walk up a steep, narrow track to a kauri grove; right is a 15-minute-return track to a lookout.

POINTS OF INTEREST

- The views from the lookout on a clear day stretch north to Ninety Mile Beach and Aupori Peninsula.
- The track also reaches a stand of youthful kauri.

7 Herekino Forest Track

GRADE 4

TIME 5 hours return

ACCESS From Kaitaia follow signs to Ahipara and after 11 km turn left at Wainui Junction into Kaitaia–Awaroa Road.

Continue 6.2 km to the summit of the hill through the Herekino Gorge. There is a parking bay on the left, from where the start of the track departs. The only indication is a small post, but a brief rummage in the bushes will suffice to find the start of the track.

TRACK NOTES

- The track is uneven but well formed and marked with orange triangles.
- It climbs via steps to the ridge and after 30 minutes the vegetation becomes more open. It crosses a saddle and after a further 45 minutes bears sharp right, descending to Rangihika Stream.
- It then climbs steeply to a ridge and after 30 minutes passes through a grove of large kauri. It then crosses another stream and after 45 minutes exits at a wide vehicle track.
- Return via the same track.

POINTS OF INTEREST

- This walk passes through a variety of forest types including verdant gullies with paritaniwha, saddles with fields of lycopodium and ridge tops of rimu and large kauri.
- The Herekino Forest was extensively logged for kauri, with driving dams transporting logs down the steep watersheds in times of flood. Bullock teams also hauled logs to the mills at Pukepoto, Herekino and Whangape. The timber was then exported from the Herekino and Whangape harbours.

Karikari Peninsula

Karikari Peninsula was formerly a collection of offshore islands, which have since been joined to the mainland by huge sandspits. It is a lonely and desolate landscape, mostly mantled by peat soils. These preserved the kauri gum that sustained a flourishing industry in the late 1800s and early 1900s.

8 Whangatupere Bay Walk

GRADE 3

TIME 3¼ hours return

ACCESS From SH 10 follow Inland Road 23 km to Maitai Bay (formerly Matai Bay). In the campground follow signs to the day-use carpark on the southern side of Maitai Point.

TRACK NOTES

- For 30 minutes follow Merita Beach around both points to a small post with an orange triangle at the far side of Poroa Stream.

- Continue to follow the stream for 30 minutes. The track is narrow, uneven and slippery but well formed and marked with orange triangles.
- At the signpost, turn left up the steep, slippery hill to Paraawanui Trig (20 minutes return). The best views are from a little past the summit.
- Retrace your steps to the signposts. After 15 minutes along a vehicle track you come to a crossroads. Turn left at the signposts, from where it is 10 minutes to Whangatupere Bay. This track narrows and becomes steeper on approaching the bay.

POINTS OF INTEREST

- Paraawanui Trig is 142 m above sea level and from the lookout the two white sand crescents of Maitai Bay look inviting.
- During the solar eclipse of 1965 several small rockets were launched from Maitai Bay by an American space investigation team in conjunction with New Zealand scientists.
- Dolphins are frequent visitors to Maitai Bay.
- Whangatupere Bay is a rocky bay with azure waters. Steep forested cliffs tumble to the water.

The vast swamps of the Karikari Peninsula were formerly the haunt of gumdiggers.

9 Puheke Recreation Reserve Walk

GRADE 2

TIME 30 minutes return

ACCESS From SH 10, follow Inland Road and continue 10.5 km, then turn left into Rangiputa Road. Then, 2 km after the turnoff to Rangiputa, turn left into Puheke Road (the road sign may not be visible). Continue to the beach along the unsealed road. The start of the track is signposted up a rough 4WD track through a gate, just before reaching the parking area near the beach.

If you don't think your vehicle will make it up the 4WD track, it is 5 minutes to the start of the walk.

TRACK NOTES For 5 minutes the track follows the metalled road to a stile. The climb is up a steep grass bank.

POINTS OF INTEREST

- Puheke Hill is the point of highest relief for a considerable distance. There are extensive views of the white sandy beaches of Karikari Bay, Puheke Bay to the east and Karikari Beach to the west. The outline of the entire Karikari Peninsula is visible with Doubtless Bay to the southeast and Rangaunu Bay to the southwest. Aupori Peninsula retreats to the distant horizon.
- Behind the beach at the base of Puheke Hill are middens containing fragments of moa eggshell. Sifting through the middens has enabled archaeologists to discover something of the culture and diet of the early inhabitants of the region.

10 Gum Hole Reserve Walk

GRADE 1

TIME 2 minutes return

ACCESS From SH 10 follow Inland Road for 2 km to a small roadside parking area. The start of the track is signposted.

TRACK NOTES The walk is metalled and even. It loops through manuka scrub growing close to the track.

POINTS OF INTEREST

- The walk passes a series of holes excavated by gum diggers. When searching for gum, the gum diggers would probe the ground with a spear to locate a piece of gum, then either dig using a spade, or work the gum up with a hook. It was often necessary to dig a pit, as in many places successive kauri forests have grown on top of each other. By digging it was easier to probe deep beneath the surface.
- The anaerobic conditions of the waterlogged peat soils preserved the gum so that it matured into a rich amber, useful in the manufacture of varnish.
- Lake Ohia at the foot of the peninsula was drained in 1900 and diggers dug drains to expose the gum. Eels some 200 mm in diameter were found when the lake was drained. Kauri stumps, since dated as 4000 years old, were discovered in the lakebed.

- A large village sprang up around the gumfield and a store was run by the Urliches, whose names are echoed in the local road names. Many grog shops were frequented by the same customers as the unofficial 'hotel'. Diggers lived in thatch shacks or 'humpies' — old jute sacks tied around a manuka frame.
- The heyday of the industry was before the First World War, but by the 1920s farming had replaced gum digging.

Omahuta Forest

At the time of writing, access to Omahuta Forest is hindered by Kauri Sanctuary Road being closed. You must therefore park on the roadside 5 km before the road-end and the entrance to Omahuta Kauri Sanctuary Walk.

To walk from the parking area to the start of the Kauri Stump Walk takes 45 minutes one way (3 km) and to the start of the Omahuta Kauri Sanctuary Walk takes 1 hour 20 minutes one way (5 km). This follows the metalled access road.

Access to Omahuta Forest is along Omahuta Road, 800 m south of Mangamuka Bridge. After 5.6 km it bears right, turning into Kauri Sanctuary Road (signposts with road names are sparse). The road is closed 2.5 km further on.

Omahuta was extensively logged in the late 1800s, the timber being flushed down the Mangamuka and Waihou rivers to the sawmill at Kohukohu. Much of the surrounding land was clearfelled and burned to establish pasture, but fortunately the rugged terrain spared some fine trees.

In 1886 Omahuta became a state forest and thus ripe for destruction with a view to settlement and farming. Over 300,000 cubic metres of timber were extracted. Every possible creek was dammed and 1 km-long chutes were constructed to swiftly transport logs down to the main dam. It was 19 km to the Hokianga Harbour from where logs were taken for milling.

More logging took place for boat building during the war effort between 1942 and 1946. Major fires in 1913 and 1931 burned huge areas and a devastating cyclone in 1959 toppled over 200 kauri.

The formation of the Omahuta Kauri Sanctuary in 1951 has preserved some of the finest trees.

11 Omahuta Kauri Sanctuary Walk

GRADE 2
TIME 30 minutes return
TRACK NOTES The track is metalled with minor undulations. It can be uneven in places.
POINTS OF INTEREST
- This majestic stand of kauri was recognised for its unique qualities, being a rare collection of large trees in close proximity. It exhibits a fine display of both mature and youthful specimens.
- Many of the largest trees have names such as Ngatuahine, Whakamakere, Taniwha, Rakaunui, Kopi, Hokianga, Tokoiwa, Tokerau and Ngapuhi. This practice of naming was common among Maori, who revered the trees.
- In 1951, 6 ha were converted into the Omahuta Kauri Sanctuary. Many of the larger trees have a girth of nearly 10 m and a height of over 50 m. The frequency of trees with a great height in the Omahuta Sanctuary is possibly because of a difference in original stock or their growth on different soils.
- Kopi, who fell in strong winds in 1973, at the time was the third largest known kauri. When he fell his trunk was hollow and, in places, as thin as the bark. He has now rotted to form a cavern. He was home to a colony of over 1000 short-tailed bats, had a girth of 13.18 m and a total height of 55.39 m.
- Hokianga is the tallest of the kauri giants and is the seventh largest tree overall. He is named after the nearby harbour and is the largest in the sanctuary. Taniwha is Northland's ninth biggest tree and means 'monster'.

12 Kauri Stump Walk

GRADE 1
TIME 5 minutes return
TRACK NOTES The track is wide, metalled and even. After the stump, the track continues 20 m to the discarded crown.
POINTS OF INTEREST
- This huge stump is nearly 5 m in diameter. It now gives life to ferns and mosses.

- You can see the remains of the scarf, which determined the direction the tree was to fall. The final cut was made at an angle, giving the top of the stump a slant. It would have taken four to six men to fell a tree of this size.
- The nearby crown was discarded and only the substantial straight bole was removed for milling.

Whangaroa

13 Wairakau Stream Track

GRADE 4

TIME 4 hours return

ACCESS Follow Totara North Road for 3 km from SH 10 and turn left into Campbell Road. The start of the track is signposted on the left after 500 m, where there is a small roadside parking bay.

TRACK NOTES

- The track is marked with orange triangles. From the parking bay follow the metalled Wairakau Road (the right fork) up the steep hill for 10 minutes past the locked gate.
- Take the track to the left that is wide but slippery when wet. After 20 minutes you come to a clearing. The track then narrows and becomes very uneven on its descent to Wairakau Stream (45 minutes).

The tentacles of Whangaroa Harbour lie at the base of the fiordesque cliffs.

- The two stream crossings are in quick succession. Wet feet are unavoidable. Do not cross the stream in times of flood. Wait until the water level subsides or return via the same track.
- For the next 45 minutes to Lane Cove Hut, the track crosses waterlogged long grass on the valley floor, side streams and slips, some of which are sizeable and muddy.
- There are toilets at Lane Cove Hut. The 16-bunk hut can be booked at DoC in Kerikeri.

POINTS OF INTEREST Whangaroa Harbour is most famous for being the scene of the burning of the *Boyd* in 1809. Local Maori offered to lead Captain John Thompson and most of the crew ashore to show them a suitable cargo of kauri spars. Out of the ship's sight they were slaughtered and their clothes donned for a later raid. During the boarding of the ship an explosion set it alight and it drifted and sunk. Of the 70 aboard, 66 died.

14 Duke's Nose (Kairara Rocks)

GRADE 4
TIME 1 hour return
ACCESS The start of the track is signposted from Lane Cove Hut.
TRACK NOTES
- The track is marked with orange triangles and climbs steadily through forest for 25 minutes.
- The final few metres involve climbing the near-vertical rock face to the summit. The matrix of stones in the rock allows for hand and foot holds to be located, but you must be capable of basic rock climbing to attempt this walk.

POINTS OF INTEREST
- The track leads to Pekapeka Bay, a many-tentacled inlet of Whangaroa Harbour. Towering bluffs and vertical cliff faces protrude through the forested valleys. The landscape resembles a miniature fiord.
- Turquoise waters blend with mangrove forests at the base of the cliffs, from where the lush forest climbs the valley sides.
- The tops of the bluffs have been weathered to form bulbous pedestals, ready to topple at any moment. The Duke's Nose is one such example. Waterfalls cascade over the cliffs and rock pinnacles tower over the headlands between coves. This is a unique Tolkienesque landscape.

15 St Paul's Rock Summit Walk

GRADE 3

TIME 45 minutes return

ACCESS Continue through Whangaroa and turn right into Old Hospital Road. This unsealed road climbs very steeply to a small turning area with limited parking.

The start of the track is signposted just before reaching the turning area.

TRACK NOTES

- The track passes through private property along the fenceline for 5 minutes. This section can be very muddy after periods of rain.
- After crossing a stile, it climbs steadily through long grass on a worn track, occasionally marked with yellow-banded green posts.
- It skirts St Paul's Rock, climbing steeply, in one section aided by a chain bolted to the rock.

POINTS OF INTEREST

- There were once two mighty gods, one named Taratara who had two wives, and Maungataniwha, a jealous and hot-tempered god, who was wifeless. When his request for one of Taratara's wives was declined, he lashed out in rage, decapitating Taratara. His head rolled across Whangaroa Harbour to Ohakiri, where it lies today, known now as St Paul's Rock.
- From the summit there are magnificent views over Whangaroa Harbour.
- Middens indicate previous Maori occupation of the area.

16 Mahinepua Peninsula Track

GRADE 3

TIME 1¾ hours return

ACCESS On Wainui Road, turn into Mahinepua Road between Wainui and Tauranga Valley. Follow it 1 km to Mahinepua Bay. The start of the track is signposted from the northern end of the beach.

TRACK NOTES

- For the first 10 minutes the track is marked with orange triangles and follows a private driveway. The Mahinepua Scenic Reserve is signposted on the right.

- After 10 minutes the track drops to two small beaches before following a ridgeline through low manuka and long grass. For the next 30 minutes to the trig, the track is narrow, uneven and, in places, overgrown. It is well formed and occasional posts show the way.
- There is a return route signposted from near the trig, which follows the north coast of the peninsula, rejoining the main track after 15 minutes.

POINTS OF INTEREST

- Mahinepua Peninsula juts out from Mahinepua Bay, which it shelters along with a selection of sandy and pebble beaches. Views west stretch to Whangaroa Bay via a succession of promontories, islets and reefs. East are the Cavalli Islands with Cape Brett in the far distance.
- Prostrate manuka grows in low clumps and *Pimelia tomentosa*, with its small accretions of tiny triangular leaflets, grow on the headland.
- Past the dwindling conclusion of the peninsula are two islands. The nearest is known as Motuekaiti (Little Flat Island) and Motueka (Flat Island). Whalers were said to congregate on Motuekaiti and the sheltered inner bays of the peninsula.
- The bay closest to Mahinepua Bay was called Piapia. One translation reads 'Beer, beer'.

The sheltered bay at Mahinepua is perfect for a swim after your walk along the peninsula.

Walks around Hokianga and Dargaville

Hokianga Harbour

17 Arai-te-uru Walk

GRADE 1

TIME 15 minutes return

ACCESS From the eastern end of Omapere, turn into Signal Station Road. The unsealed road leads to a parking area from where the start of the track is signposted.

TRACK NOTES

- The track is metalled, even and signposted. It performs a loop around the South Head of Hokianga Harbour.
- There is a further 10-minute-return walk from the carpark, which winds down a grass bank on a well-formed track to a beach at the base of the hill.

POINTS OF INTEREST

- Arai-te-uru is the name given to the South Head of Hokianga Harbour. According to Maori mythology, Niua, at the North Head, and Arai-te-uru were two taniwha Kupe left to guide the returning waka of Ngatokimatawhaorua and Mamari many years later.
- In 1838, John Martin bought the headland and constructed a signalling mast on the point to help guide ships over the treacherous bar, which has claimed over 20 vessels. His farmhouse was located 2 miles away on the hill and was painted white to act as a navigation marker.
- In 1867 the Marine Department was established and the original flagstaff was modified to incorporate a cross arm, which carried discs indicating the state of the tide. In 1898 a white light was added.

Waipoua Forest

When the eminent botanist Leonard Cockayne surveyed the Waipoua Forest in 1908, he identified 241 species and called it 'a forest museum …

one of the noblest forests'. He concluded that if the park was saved from milling 'it would constitute one of the great sights of the world'. Nearly 100 years later, his foresight has been proved correct.

Today, the Waipoua Forest contains the greatest abundance of kauri of the most massive proportions. The forest is home to Tane Mahuta, Te Matua Ngahere and other notable trees, most of which are accessible by a series of good walking tracks.

The area around present-day Waipoua was built up around 25 million years ago in a submarine environment over layers of sandstone sediment and stony deposits. Fifteen million years ago these strata were submerged beneath volcanic lava flows, derived from a chain of volcanoes to the west of today's coastline. More layers of sediment accumulated before tectonic forces uplifted the whole region. Most of the area near the coast was covered in substantial dunes around two million years ago, which were dissected by streams and sandy terraces.

The sandy topsoil under the kauri is of low fertility with impermeable iron and silica pans. Many soils of the region are strongly leached under the burden of over 2200 mm annual rainfall.

Waipoua Forest is New Zealand's largest remaining tract of unmodified mature kauri forest. This distinctive forest type has several species associations such as kauri-taraire, which was first noted by Leonard Cockayne in 1908.

Kauri grass, hangehange, neinei, kiekie and ferns are common in the understorey. Kohekohe prevails on the high plateau.

The forest is home to the largest population of North Island brown kiwi and the rare nocturnal, carnivorous kauri snail.

The local people are Te Roroa, meaning 'tall ones', who lived on shellfish, fish, forest resources and a well-developed agriculture. They used the alluvial terraces to grow kumara, taro and bracken roots.

The Waipoua Forest contains the largest tract of unmodified kauri forest in New Zealand.

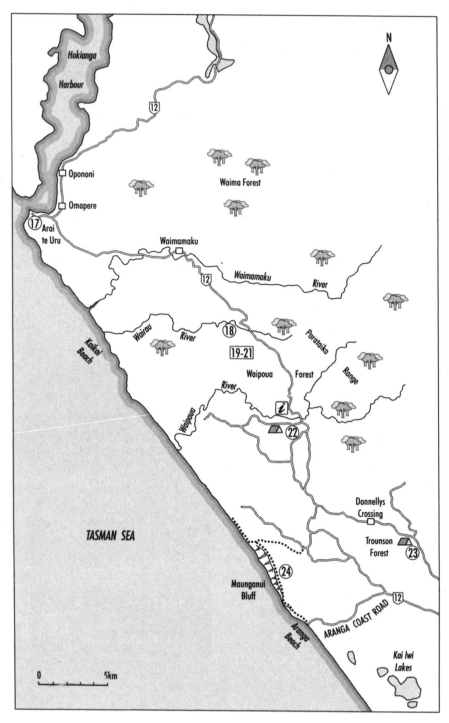

N

Hokianga
Harbour

Opononi

Omapere

17 Arai
te Uru

Waima Forest

Waimamaku

12

Waimamaku River

Wairau River

18

19-21

Waipoua Forest

Paratuiko Range

Waipoua River

Kaikai Beach

i

22

TASMAN SEA

Donnellys
Crossing

Trounson
Forest

23

24

Maunganui
Bluff

Aranga Beach

ARANGA COAST ROAD

12

Kai Iwi
Lakes

0   5km

Waipoua

The original Waipoua Block of 35,300 acres (14,285 ha) was purchased by the Crown for £4400 in 1876 from chiefs Parore Te Awha and Tiopira Kinaki. Debate ensued as to whether the area should be used for farming or forestry.

Waipoua survived logging because of its inaccessibility. Neither the Waipoua nor Waimamaku rivers were large enough to transport logs. However, by the Second World War, roads were improved enough for some kauri extraction for use in the construction of patrol boats for the US Navy.

Subsequent pressure to remove all the kauri and convert the land to pasture was thwarted with the formation of the Waipoua Preservation Society. It mobilised nationwide support and collected around 70,000 signatures in a petition presented to Parliament. In 1952, 9105 ha were set aside when the Waipoua Forest Sanctuary was established.

The Yakas Kauri, Four Sisters and Te Matua Ngahere can all be explored from the same parking area. It takes approximately 7 minutes to walk to the junction, from where the three tracks depart. Subtract 15 minutes from a return journey on each of these walks if you want to explore all the trees on one trip.

All the tracks around the base of kauri have elaborate boardwalks. These not only provide an agreeable walking surface, but also protect the shallow and vulnerable roots of the trees. Keep to the tracks.

18 Tane Mahuta

GRADE 1

TIME 5 minutes return

ACCESS Tane Mahuta is comprehensively signposted on SH 12, 11 km north of the Waipoua Visitor Centre. There are toilets, picnic tables and roadside parking nearby.

TRACK NOTES

- The track is wide, metalled, even and suitable for wheelchairs, although one fallen tree at an angle over the track may need negotiation.
- Boardwalks protect the shallow fragile root systems of the tree.

POINTS OF INTEREST

- In Maori mythology, Tane was the son of Ranginui (Sky Father) and Papatuanuku (Earth Mother). With his almighty strength he separated their embrace, creating light, air and space — the elements for life to flourish. Tane is thus seen as the life giver and all living creatures are his progeny.

- Tane Mahuta, God of the Forest, is estimated to be 2000 years old. He is 51.5 m high, with a girth of 13.8 m. He rises nearly 10 m before there is any tapering in his trunk. He is the largest and best-known kauri. The largest ever-recorded kauri had a girth nearly twice as large.

- The dying tips of his branches show Tane Mahuta is in the autumn of his years and probably hollowing on the inside. His sheltered location should allow for continued wonder for generations yet.

- Over 15 percent of the recorded species in the Waipoua Forest live as an empire of epiphytes in the clefts between Tane Mahuta's upper branches. Moisture collects in these hollows and a moss begins to form. This creates an embryonic soil for a seed, either blown by the wind or dropped by a bird, to germinate. The leaf litter accumulates and develops humus, sustaining the plant. In this way a hanging garden evolves in the tree.

19 Four Sisters Track

GRADE 1

TIME 20 minutes return

ACCESS The kauri walks are signposted 11 km north of Waipoua River Road and 1 km south of Tane Mahuta on SH 12. There is a large parking area where your vehicle will be guarded for a small fee.

TRACK NOTES

- From the carpark follow the wide, even and metalled track for 7 minutes to the three-way junction. The Four Sisters are signposted on the right. A boardwalk circumnavigates the trees.

POINTS OF INTEREST

- The Four Sisters sprout from the same base, although some may be growing at the expense of others. It is thought trees grow in close proximity because of the heavy seeds, which are wind blown and travel only a short distance from the parent tree. Kauri forests have a scattering of twin kauri and a few triplets. An example of four mature trees growing from a shared base is very rare.

20 Te Matua Ngahere

GRADE 2

TIME 45 minutes return

ACCESS The kauri walks are signposted 11 km north of Waipoua River Road and 1 km south of Tane Mahuta on SH 12. There is a large parking area where your vehicle will be guarded for a small fee.

TRACK NOTES

- From the carpark follow the wide, even, metalled track for 7 minutes to the three-way junction.
- Te Matua Ngahere is signposted straight ahead. The track continues to be metalled with substantial boardwalks.

POINTS OF INTEREST

- Te Matua Ngahere means 'Father of the forest'. The enormous bulk of the trunk and crowded clefts of the decaying upper branches emit a stately atmosphere. To be in the presence of this tree is a humbling experience.
- His girth is the greatest of all kauri at 16.41 m. His squat appearance relates to a height of 29.87 m.

Gracing the upper canopy with a monumental presence, Te Matua Ngahere is a formidable tree.

He is probably hollow on the inside. Measured by the quantity of merchantable timber, he is the second-largest known kauri.

21 Yakas Kauri Track

GRADE 2

TIME 1¼ hours return

ACCESS The kauri walks are signposted 11 km north of Waipoua River Road and 1 km south of Tane Mahuta on SH 12. There is a large parking area where your vehicle will be guarded for a small fee.

TRACK NOTES

- From the carpark follow the wide, even and metalled track for 7 minutes to the three-way junction. The Yakas Track is signposted on the left.
- The track continues to be wide and metalled with extensive boardwalks for the 30 minutes to the Cathedral Grove and Yakas Kauri.

POINTS OF INTEREST

- The Cathedral Grove is a stand of mature kauri just before the Yakas Kauri. The reverence of the tall pillars and the monumental size of their trunks lends an ecclesiastical feel to the forest, reminiscent of a large cathedral.
- The Yakas Kauri is the seventh-largest known tree in New Zealand, with a girth of 12.29 m and clean bole of 9.75 m. Its height is 43.89 m.
- The tree was discovered by Nick Yakas, a former bushman and gum climber. He arrived in New Zealand as a teenager in 1903 from Dalmatia. Hard working and industrious, he soon became an expert climber with weighted line and hooks, scaling trees with remarkable nimbleness.
- While working in the Waipoua Forest during the logging days, he remembered a large tree that may have rivalled the dimensions of the visited giants. On a sortie

The presence of the Yakas Kauri pervades the vicinity of the forest it occupies.

with Alfred Reed, noted walker and publisher, Tudor Collins, the celebrated photographer of the logging era, and Ellen Weck, they located the tree in 1966.

22 Lookout Track

GRADE 3

TIME 2½ hours return

ACCESS The start of the track is signposted 300 m before the Waipoua Visitor Centre on Waipoua River Road. There is limited roadside parking, so it is better to park by the Visitor Centre. Alternatively, you can reach the lookout tower by turning into Waipoua Settlement Road 5.6 km south of Waipoua River Road and following it 4.1 km.

TRACK NOTES

- The track is well formed and marked with orange triangles. In places it is uneven and muddy. It climbs gently to a lookout tower above Waipoua Valley.

POINTS OF INTEREST

- The tower was originally used as a lookout to observe the surrounding areas for fires. It commands extensive views to the coast, Mt Hauturu and the Parataiko Range to the east. The distinctive crowns of kauri cap the ridge tops.
- From the elevated vantage point, interpretive panels explain the geology and ecology of the area. The tower has a sheltered interior and an exterior balcony around the perimeter.

The watchtower at the top of the Lookout Track was formerly used to scan the forest for fires.

23 Trounson Kauri Park

GRADE 1

TIME 40 minutes return

ACCESS Trounson Kauri Park is signposted from SH 12 along Kaitui Road from the north (8 km) and Trounson Park Road from the south (7 km). There is a DoC campground (open only in summer) and toilets nearby. The track entrance is signposted 100 m from the junction with Mangatu Road along Trounson Park Road, where there is a large parking area.

TRACK NOTES

- The track is wide, even and metalled. It performs a loop through the forest, over a substantial boardwalk and alongside a stream.
- Information panels and two poetic auditory accompaniments give information on the kauri and ecology of the forest.

POINTS OF INTEREST

- In 1890 James Trounson set aside 3.14 ha of land for a reserve and added 21.45 ha later. Before the park was officially opened in 1921 a further 367 ha were added. The total area now comprises 457 ha.
- The forests of Northland are presided over by a conspicuous, eerie quietness that is only broken by the occasional chuckling of a stream or the rustling of foliage in the wind. The rush of wings or the melancholy tunes of the forests' avian residents are sadly absent.
- Bird numbers have been crushed to low levels by stoats, ferrets and cats; loss of habitat through land clearance for farming and exotic forestry; and competition for food from possums and rats. Some populations are below the threshold needed to survive.
- The mainland island concept was introduced to preserve environments where predator numbers are controlled through trapping and poisoning. The native plant species are given a chance to proliferate, supplying an abundant food resource to the native birds.
- Species such as North Island brown kiwi, New Zealand pigeon, bats and kauri snail now have recovering populations in Trounson's protected confines.
- Kauri grow prolifically on the reserve in symmetrical columns of untapering beauty. They grow in dense stands and are sometimes the only tree in a particular area of forest.

24 Maunganui Bluff Walk

GRADE 4

TIME 2½ hours return

ACCESS From SH 12 south of Aranga, turn into unsealed Aranga Coast Road and follow it 6 km to the beach. The start of the track is signposted on the right by a small parking bay.

TRACK NOTES

- For 20 minutes the narrow track passes through dense thickets of flax, before entering coastal forest. It climbs steadily for 30 minutes and is marked with orange triangles. It then follows a fenceline for 10 minutes before veering left up a vehicle track for 10 minutes to the trig at the summit.

POINTS OF INTEREST

- Maunganui Bluff rises to nearly 500 m above sea level and protrudes from a tumultuous sea in sheer cliffs. Hardy flax clings in clefts, but little other vegetation can gain hold. On the lee side of the bluff is a verdant coastal forest of nikau, puriri, taraire and kohekohe.

- Large puriri grow on the high cliff frontage. The shrub napuka (*Hebe speciosa*) still grows in its natural environment on the slopes, and snow grass, which is usually confined to the South Island, flourishes here on the northern coastline.
- Views from the summit stretch endlessly in all directions. To the south, the white-capped breakers of Ripiro Beach retreat to a blur on the salt-laden horizon. To the north lie the low former dunes of the Waipoua coast and to the east the Tutamoe Range.
- Maori say Maunganui Bluff looks towards Kaipara and they used it as a vantage point. Ngati Whatua, whose boundary once lay in the vicinity of the bluff, used smoke signals from the highest point as an early warning system to communicate to more southerly tribes the danger of impending attack.
- Around the beginning of the 1800s, when Ngapuhi passed down the coast, chiefs Murupaenga and Taoho, who lived near present-day Baylys Beach, were warned of Hongi Hika's approaching war party. They were able to defeat it by ambush.

25 Tokatoka Scenic Reserve Walk

GRADE 3
TIME 20 minutes return
ACCESS From Dargaville, follow SH 12 for 17 km south to Tokatoka and turn left into Tokatoka Road (unsealed). Follow it 1 km to a small parking bay on the left, from where the start of the track is signposted.
TRACK NOTES
- The worn track climbs steadily through a low forest canopy. In places it is steep and can be very slippery, especially on the way down.
POINTS OF INTEREST
- The conical shape of Tokatoka is the eroded stump of a former volcanic cone. It lies as a prominent high point in the vast flood plain of the Wairoa River, which threads a sinuous course past the peak. The Tutamoe Range and Tangihua Range are visible on the distant horizon to the northeast.
- Tokatoka is associated with chief Taoho of Te Roroa hapu around the beginning of the 1800s. The impregnable site was witness to smoke

signals from Maunganui Bluff, warning of Hongi Hika's approaching war party. With his Ngati Whatua warriors, he was able to ambush and defeat the invaders.

- After a visit to Ripiro Beach to feed on toheroa, five mountain brothers, who had journeyed from the east, tried valiantly to re-cross the mighty Wairoa River. Tokatoka and Maungaraho crossed, and waited for Motu-wheteke to pluck up the courage. Okiri-ahi struggled, drowned and became a reef. Te Kewi-pahu-tai only just made the crossing and stands on the river's edge. This legend explains some of the sacred hills in the region.

26 Kauri Bushmen's Memorial Walk

GRADE 1

TIME 10 minutes return

ACCESS 3.6 km from Matakohe and 6 km from Paparoa on SH 12, turn into Sterling Road. The start of the walk is signposted on the left by a small parking bay, 1.7 km further on.

TRACK NOTES

- The track is even but with a slight gradient. It performs a loop through the forest.

POINTS OF INTEREST

- At the entrance to the track is a log hauler, used to transport logs carried by teams of bullocks on primitive bush roads.
- The reserve was purchased in 1954 as a memorial to the pre-First World War kauri bushmen. Although the industry is remembered as one of destruction and flagrant demolition of a majestic species, it was also a time of high human endeavour. Bushmen living in harsh conditions and in rugged country developed kinship and camaraderie, not to mention an affection for their environment (despite its plunder).
- Observe forested ridges as you pass through an area of former kauri forest. There will often be a solitary large tree still occupying the ridge, left by the bushmen for the continuation of the species.
- The dense stand of kauri on the hilltop has a regenerating understorey of kohekohe, red matipo and a carpet of hound's tongue fern.

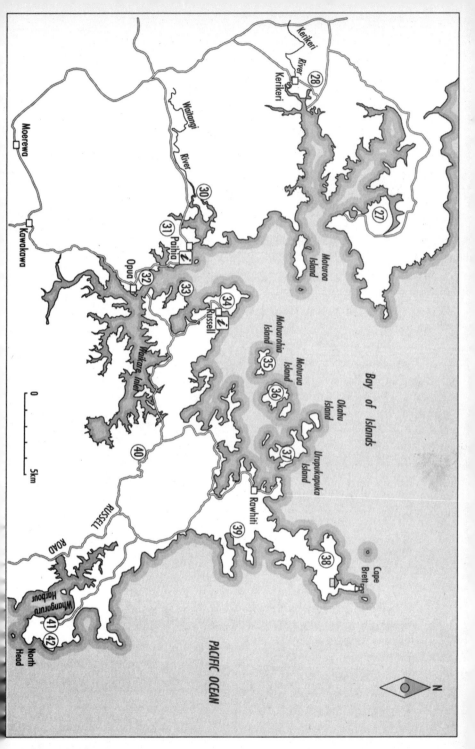

The Bay of Islands walks.

Walks around Bay of Islands and Whangaruru

Kerikeri

27 Marsden Cross Historic Reserve Walk

GRADE 2

TIME 1 hour return

ACCESS Turn into Kapiro Road, just south of Kapiro and north of Waipapa on SH 10 near Kerikeri. Kapiro Road can also be accessed from Kerikeri by following signs to Purerua after passing through the Kerikeri Basin.

Turn into Purerua Road and follow it to the junction with Rangihoua Road and bear left. The walking access through Mataka Station is signposted on the left 5.6 km from the junction.

TRACK NOTES

- The walk follows a metalled and even farm road for 20 minutes before crossing a stile and descending steadily to Rangihoua Bay (10 minutes), sometimes referred to as Oihi Bay.
- Around the reserve may be muddy.

POINTS OF INTEREST

- The Reverend Samuel Marsden preached the first Christian sermon in New Zealand at Oihi Bay on Christmas Day in 1814.
- He had purchased the brig *Active* to shuttle between Port Jackson in New South Wales and New Zealand. Marsden landed on 22 December with three lay

Samuel Marsden preached the first Christian sermon in New Zealand from the brig of the *Active* at Oihi Bay.

missionaries, Kendall, Hall and King. Together with Hongi Hika and his nephew Ruatara, Samuel Marsden conducted a service, which Ruatara translated to the many Maori gathered.

- New Zealand's first mission was established near the site and although protected by Hongi Hika, they found living tough in miserable winter conditions, with a lack of timber and arable land. They ended up trading muskets for food.
- A nearby headstone marks the memory of those buried in the area from the Rangihoua Mission, which occupied the site from 1814 to 1854.
- Nearby is a memorial anchor to Thomas and Elizabeth Hansen, first non-missionary settlers in New Zealand, who arrived in February 1816.

28 Kororipo Pa Walk

GRADE 1

TIME 20 minutes return

ACCESS Park at the designated parking area in the Kerikeri Basin, 50 m after passing over the bridge.

Retrace your steps over the bridge, past the Old Stone Store to where the start of the track is signposted on the left.

TRACK NOTES The track is metalled and even. It climbs gently to the pa, where you can walk over the grassed area to the interpretive panels.

POINTS OF INTEREST

- Kororipo pa commands a prominent position on a hill between a bend in the Kerikeri River and the Wairoa Stream. The name 'Kororipo' was used only after 1828 and means 'a whirlpool', relating to the tidal flow on the inlet below.
- Hongi Hika's grandfather Auha had ousted Ngati Kahu from Kerikeri around 1760 and took possession of Kororipo. Its prime location close to abundant fishing grounds and shellfish sites later was enhanced by being close to European ships for trading.
- The pa is surrounded on three sides by water and extensive, uncrossable mangrove swamps. A deep ditch and sturdy palisade defended the pa.
- The pa was known as Te Wara o te Riki — The inlet of war — following Hongi Hika's visit to England. He accompanied his friend the Reverend Thomas Kendall and collaborated with Professor Lee of Cambridge in clarifying the vocabulary and grammar of the Maori language, which was previously undocumented.

- He received many gifts on account of his lively personality and polite demeanour, including a suit of armoured mail from King George IV. The return trip passed through Sydney, where Hongi Hika traded many of his acquisitions for around 300 muskets. On his return to New Zealand, he sent war parties over the upper North Island.
- In September 1821 a war party of 50 canoes and hundreds of muskets left Kororipo pa to raid tribes in the Hauraki region. Later parties slaughtered tribes in the Waikato, Rotorua, Bay of Plenty, East Cape and Kaipara, all of whom had no access to muskets. They enlisted slaves who worked on the productive land in the Kerikeri Basin. The Musket Wars continued until 1827, when Hongi Hika was shot (not wearing his suit of armour) and later died in 1828.
- Information panels explain how the pa may have looked and functioned, with descriptions of the defence systems and methods of building construction.

The Kerikeri River provided a strategic and defendable location for Kororipo pa.

29 Manginangina Kauri Walk

GRADE 1

TIME 10 minutes return

ACCESS From SH 1 near Kerikeri, follow Puketotara Road, then turn right onto Waiare Road (unsealed). The start of the walk is signposted 6.5 km on the left, 1.5 km after the Puketi Recreation Area. There are two parking bays close by.

Puketi Kauri Forest is also signposted off SH 10 on Waiare Road 2 km south of Kaeo.

TRACK NOTES The elevated boardwalk weaves a sinuous path through the forest. It is suitable for wheelchairs.

POINTS OF INTEREST

- Interpretive panels explain the ecology of the forest and kauri, which are the feature of this walk.
- Various growth stages of the kauri are visible, indicating how the form of the tree changes. After the early 'ricker' stage, when the kauri exhibits a pyramidal form, it develops a solid columnar trunk. Its lower branches are shed and its graceful crown opens to capture the light. Once established the tree continues to gain bulk until, after millennia, it benevolently fades.
- A number of trees fell during a devastating cyclone in 1959.
- The name Manginangina means 'in and out of sight'. Maori used the nearby hill as a lookout to watch approaching canoes on the indented coastline.
- Some of the trees show scars left from the days when taps were cut into the bark to bleed gum. A bushman would return months later to recover the lumps of valuable sap that formed around the wounds. This practice was later banned (but never policed) because of the harm it caused to the trees.
- Kokako and kiwi sometimes roam the reserve although meetings now occur with unfortunate rarity.

Paihia

30 Haruru Falls Track/Waitangi National Trust Mangrove Walk

GRADE 2

TIME 2 hours one way

ACCESS The walk starts from the northern end of the Waitangi National Trust Park, opposite the Waitangi Trust Visitor Centre. This is the nearest carpark.

Alternatively, if attempting the walk in reverse, follow Puketona Road from Paihia for 5 km and turn right into Haruru Falls Road. There is a carpark on the right after the bridge over the Waitangi River.

TRACK NOTES

- Initially the track skirts the golf course (follow the yellow marker posts), before passing through a turnstile. Through the kanuka forest the track is wide and well formed but unmetalled.
- After 1 hour the track crosses an arm of the estuary on a boardwalk, which continues for approximately 20 minutes through the mangroves. It can be slippery when wet.
- At the end of the boardwalk, turn left. The track skirts the shoreline of the Waitangi River before exiting through a turnstile. There is a 2-minute walk from the carpark at the Haruru Falls to a lookout over the falls.

POINTS OF INTEREST

- The elegantly constructed boardwalk through the mangroves provides the ideal way to explore this unique habitat, which is otherwise inaccessible by foot.
- Mangroves (*Avicennia marina* ssp. *australasica*) are uniquely adapted to their harsh environment. Their shallow radial roots anchor well in the anaerobic muds and protect the trees from strong winds and tidal scours. Vertical breathing roots, known as pneumatophores, are exposed at low tide and enable the trees to transpire.
- The leaves have a waxy topside, which reflects the strong light, and a downy coat of fine hairs on their underside retards the loss of water through transpiration. Mangrove seeds germinate on the tree and the

Haruru Falls Track/Waitangi National Trust Mangrove Walk.

seedpods can be carried on tidal currents for up to four months while the seed remains viable.

- Mangroves are important indicators of the ecological health of an estuary. They reoxygenate the water and provide habitat for molluscs, crustaceans, up to 30 fish species and numerous wading birds.
- After the boardwalk, the native vegetation sequence is exhibited on the estuary, from mangroves to salt marshes to coastal scrub.
- The Haruru Falls form a picturesque crescent and drain the Waitangi River. Before the advent of Europeans, horses and bridle tracks, the Waitangi River was the main Maori communications route. Haruru Falls represented the entrance to the Bay of Islands.
- Haruru was a busy port in the late 1800s, exporting timber, kauri gum, cattle, dairy produce, sheep and wool.

31 Opua Forest Lookout Track

GRADE 2
TIME 1 hour return
ACCESS From Paihia town centre, follow School Road for 700 m. Just before it bears sharp right, the start of the track is signposted on the left.
TRACK NOTES

- After following the Opua Stream, the track climbs a ridge to the lookout. It is wide and well formed. After approximately 25 minutes the track forks; right takes you to the lookout, left to the Oromahoe Traverse.

POINTS OF INTEREST

- As nearby Paihia was among the first place in New Zealand settled by Europeans, the demand for timber stretches back to the mid-1800s. Kauri was first logged and taken to the Waitangi River. During the 1920s tanekaha was felled for its bark, useful in the tanning of leather. Later rimu and totara timber were taken for their attractive grain and colour. Fires and grazing also contributed to the forest's demise.
- Opua Forest is now a regenerating remnant of its former glory. The lush streamside vegetation is hung with supplejack vines. On climbing the ridge, the canopy of kanuka shades abundant tanekaha and rimu seedlings. Hangehange and coprosmas predominate in the understorey.
- The views from the lookout are extensive, from Paihia to the wider Bay of Islands.

The Opua Forest was formerly well used by Maori and early settlers travelling between farms and settlements in the region.

- The tracks in Opua Forest follow old communications routes. Pack tracks and bridle tracks were used by loggers and gum diggers and linked early farms and settlements.

32 Opua to Paihia Coastal Walkway

GRADE 2

TIME 2½ hours one way

ACCESS The track starts from the Opua Wharf and finishes at the southern end of Paihia Beach, where Marsden Road turns into Seaview Road.

TRACK NOTES

- This track is administered by the Far North District Council.
- The initial Opua Hall section of the track is closed due to slumping. It is negotiable at low tide or use the Richardson Street entry as your start point.
- The track is carved into the banks above the shoreline. It can be slippery when wet and prone to erosion. It skirts numerous small bays and headlands before entering Harrison Scenic Reserve. The track is then shaded and climbs to an elevated position above the headland.
- Crossing the Waimangaro River on a boardwalk, it passes through the motor camp. After the next headland it crosses the causeway alongside

SH 1 (Seaview Road) and weaves through Sullivan's Bay to a stone wharf, finishing at the southern end of Paihia Beach.

- Toilets are located at Opua Wharf, the northern end of Seaview Road causeway and the corner of Seaview and Marsden roads.

POINTS OF INTEREST

- This coastal walk encompasses all the beauty the Bay of Islands has to offer without the hordes of tourists. It meanders through idyllic bays and looks out to sailing boats moored in the calm, clear waters.
- From barnacle-encrusted rocky headlands there are sweeping vistas of the bay. Charming coves are lined with multicoloured boats and sprinkled with secluded homes.

Russell

33 Toretore Island Walk

GRADE 2

TIME 30 minutes return

ACCESS From Russell, follow Russell Road towards Okiato and after 6 km turn right into Te Wahapu Road. Follow it 3 km to the road-end. Toretore Island is signposted from a small parking bay.

TRACK NOTES

- Toretore Island is connected to the mainland at mid–low tide via a shingle bank.
- Head towards the end of the point for 5 minutes along the rocky foreshore to Toretore Island.
- On the island a wide, well-formed track traverses its length, terminating in a steep bluff. There are a few, sometimes slippery, rocks to negotiate.
- Return by the same route.

POINTS OF INTEREST

- Toretore Island is situated between Paihia and Russell and provides fine views.
- In Te Wahapu Bay, a trading post and ship repair yard were established by Gilbert Mair in 1831. His house stood on the point next to the Norfolk Island pine planted by his wife. Toretore was nicknamed 'Nobby', probably by one of the Mairs' children.

- Toretore Island causes confusion when the total number of islands in the bay need to be counted as at high tide it is an island and at low tide it's joined to the mainland by a causeway.

34 Flagstaff Hill

GRADE 2

TIME 45 minutes return

ACCESS From the northern end of the Strand in Russell you can walk over the rocks at mid–low tide to Watering Bay (5 minutes). The start of the track is signposted through Kororareka Scenic Reserve.

At high tide, continue 500 m up Wellington Street to a signpost on the left. After 5 minutes the even track joins the low-tide track in the Kororareka Scenic Reserve.

TRACK NOTES

- The metalled, even track climbs gently through regenerating forest for 10 minutes, exiting at Titore Way.
- Bear right and after 5 minutes the final 5 minutes to Flagstaff Hill is signposted.
- To return you can descend to the carpark between Flagstaff Hill and the lookout, from where a return to Russell is signposted along Wellington Street (15 minutes).

POINTS OF INTEREST

- Hone Heke was one of the first chiefs to sign the Treaty of Waitangi, but quickly became disillusioned with the new laws of the colony. He decided to target the symbol of British power and in July 1844, with his followers, cut down the flagstaff. After its re-erection in January 1845 Hone Heke cut it down himself.
- The threats of the guarding warriors of Chief Tamati Waka Nene were brushed off by Hone as he cut the pole down for a third time. The men didn't want to be held responsible for killing a chief, so chose not to interfere.
- After the construction of a blockhouse, Hone enlisted the help of Kawiti, who created a diversion while Hone cut the pole for a fourth time. This action led to Kororareka (Russell) being sacked and the defeat of Kawiti at Ruapekapeka. Both chiefs later surrendered to the British forces.

- When the flagpole was re-erected, the lower section was enclosed with iron.
- Flagstaff Hill is nearly 100 m above sea level and commands 360-degree views of the Bay of Islands.

35 Motuarohia Island Track

GRADE 2

TIME 20 minutes return

ACCESS The information centres in Russell and Paihia can advise on the tour operators who run boat services to the island.

TRACK NOTES The track is even and climbs to a lookout platform. The final section has been aided by the construction of elaborate wooden steps.

POINTS OF INTEREST

- The views from the summit in all directions show the splendour of the Bay of Islands.
- Motuarohia Island was originally two separate islands, which are now connected by a tombolo, or sandspit. On the southern side is an uninterrupted beach, which stretches the length of the sandspit. On the northern side three shallow lagoons enclosed by rocky islets have deeply scalloped the coastline causing the beaches to back on to the southern beach. These lagoons are ideal for snorkelling and DoC has constructed an interpretive snorkel trail with underwater plaques.
- On 29 November 1769, Captain Cook and his men landed on Motuarohia. He noted the island was numerously populated and substantially cultivated. On being surrounded by a large party of threatening Maori, Cook ordered a shot to be fired at the young chief leading the party, causing them to retreat.
- The island is also called Roberton Island and is named after John Roberton, who lived here from 1839. He purchased the island from chiefs Warerahi, Meko and Rewa, built a house and established a farm. After he drowned in 1840, a fate coincidentally shared by his five brothers, his widow stayed on the island.

  With a servant named Thomas Bull, Mrs Robertson cared for Motuarohia, her three children and Maketu, the son of a Kororareka chief. A moody and lazy boy, proud of his high standing and noble lineage, he resented their rebuking after instances of mischief. He killed all five island residents and for his murderous deed was taken to Auckland and hanged.

36 Moturua Island Track

GRADE 3

TIME 2½ hours return

ACCESS The information centres in Russell and Paihia can provide details on the tour operators who run boats to Moturua Island.

TRACK NOTES

- The track is well formed and passes through long grass, forest and beaches. It is occasionally marked with green posts.
- The walk divides into four sections, each taking 20 to 30 minutes and climbing a low hill between beaches.
- From the eastern end of Waipao Bay, climb the low hill to Otupono Bay. On the way to Waiwhapuku Bay, look for the kumara storage pits on the trackside.
- The track to Mangahawea Bay can be muddy and slippery, but the shorter section back to Waipao Bay is firmer.
- From Waipao Bay, there is a 15-minute-return walk, which departs from the eastern end of the beach and climbs to Pupuha pa.

POINTS OF INTEREST

- Captain Cook landed at Waipao Bay in 1769, where he replenished water casks.
- From 11 May 1772, Marion du Fresne and his French expedition camped on Moturua. In desperate need of water and supplies and with fatigued sailors, Waipao Bay quickly became a hospital camp. A forge was constructed to aid the substantial repairs needed to the vessels *Mascarin* and *Marquis de Castries*. They made reconnaissance trips for new masts and felled kauri spars in Clendon Cove under the command of M. Crozet.

  During their time in the Bay of Islands they took detailed notes on the Maori villages and were greeted warmly in return for their kindliness. There was a constant exchange of gifts of shellfish and fish. The French renamed Moturua Island, Marion Island.

  Relations deteriorated with Maori when clothing and a musket were stolen from the camp. Wariness of the Maori, who vastly outnumbered the sick crew, increased despite du Fresne's confidence.

While on a fishing trip to Orokawa Bay, du Fresne and his crew were killed. Subsequently, under the assumed command of M. Crozet, the hospital camp on Moturua was evacuated. Later battles were fought, with 26 French crew armed with loaded muskets causing the evacuation of a pa. They destroyed many abandoned villages, where they found the bloodstained clothes of their fellow seamen and evidence of cannibal feasts. It is suggested fishing in tapu grounds and cutting of firewood on burial sites contributed to the decline of good relations between Maori and 'Marion's Tribe'.

On 12 July 1772, New Zealand, known to the French as 'Austral France', was formally claimed for France. The officers of the two ships buried a bottle at Waipao Bay. It took them 10 months to limp back to France.

- During the Second World War, the control base for mines laid in the Bay of Islands area was situated at Waiwhapuku Bay. Remains of the housing and camp buildings are still evident here and on Pupuha pa.

37 Urupukapuka Island Track

GRADE 3
TIME 4½ hours return
ACCESS The information centres in Russell and Paihia can advise on the tour operators running services to Urupukapuka Island. Most will stop at Otehei Bay, from where the start of the walk is signposted at the southern side of the bay.
TRACK NOTES
- The track forms two loops, both of which are marked with green poles with a yellow band at the top. Climb the hill behind Otehei Bay to the signpost. Right is the shorter loop and takes 1½ hours via Cable Bay. Left explores the main portion of the island and takes approximately 3 hours.
- Both tracks follow the perimeter of the island, with occasional short detours to information panels explaining the archaeological interpretation of pa sites and other features of interest.
- The walks undulate over worn grassed tracks, and the shorter loop is grazed by sheep. The main section of the walk weaves between open grassed areas and regenerating manuka, occasionally dropping

to the beaches. Near the northern part of the island it follows the cliff top.

- After passing through Otiao Bay (Indico Bay) there is a 30-minute-return detour to Oneura Bay (Paradise Bay). The track rejoins the main route over the hill to Otehei Bay, where there is a cafe with toilets.

POINTS OF INTEREST

- The intimate island views are a microcosm of the Bay of Islands, with cliff-top pa sites capped in coastal vegetation, steep hillsides, idyllic sheltered beaches, rocky islets and reefs, and clear turquoise water.
- In a relatively confined area is a series of Maori archaeological sites with noticeable associations. The archaeological walk circumnavigates the island, with information panels at many locations bringing to life the visible remnants of the past.
- In 1772, Marion du Fresne and his ill-fated French expedition noted many villages with palisades. These were probably inhabited by Ngare Raumati people. In the early 1800s after skirmishes with Ngapuhi and Ngatirehia, kainga, or unfortified villages, still abound on the island.
- During the late 1800s the land was cleared for grazing, an activity that still continues today to minimise the fire risk.
- There are 66 archaeological sites on the island, including eight pa. The terraces, ditches, storage pits and remnant fortifications are clearly distinguishable and 14 sites are spread around the 208 hectares. Eight sites have interpretive panels.
- In 1926, American fisherman extraordinaire and writer Zane Grey established a fishing camp at Otehei Bay. He set up tents and ventured into the bay with locals to catch the elusive marlin, a fish that before that time was little caught. A more permanent fishing camp was later established, which attracted a list of wealthy clients.
- Indico Bay was named after Doro Indico, an Italian immigrant married to a New Zealander. They lived in a shanty beside the creek in the 1920s and 1930s, fishing and growing vegetables and tomatoes.

38 Cape Brett Track

GRADE 4

TIME 6½ hours one way

ACCESS From Russell, follow Russell Road and then turn left into Kempthorne Road towards Rawhiti. This runs into Manawaora Road. At the junction with Rawhiti Road, turn left and the start of the track is signposted from Hauai Bay, just after Rawhiti.

Secure parking is available from Hartwells, Kaimarama Bay, at the end of Rawhiti Road, 1 km from the start of the track.

TRACK NOTES

- The Cape Brett Hut is an old lighthouse-keeper's house and has undergone major internal renovations to convert it to a 21-person hut. You must book and pay in advance with DoC Russell to obtain the combination and for further information on the facilities provided. They can also provide up-to-date information on the track conditions.
- A track maintenance fee must also be paid prior to your departure.
- Day walkers should contact the information centres in Russell or Paihia for details of operators who can collect you by boat from Cape Brett.
- The track is wide, well formed and marked with orange triangles. The surface is mostly uneven, occasionally muddy and always on a gradient.
- For the first hour the track climbs steadily and steeply to a picnic table with magnificent views of the Bay of Islands.
- Over the next 45 minutes the track passes the junctions of tracks to Whangamumu and passes through a gate in the electric fence.
- After a further 2½ hours, a 45-minute-return detour is signposted to Deep Water Cove.
- Thirty minutes later the track exits the regenerating forest and looks out towards the tip of Cape Brett. The 1½ hours to the lighthouse crosses grassland. In places the track is perched on a knife-edge with steep cliffs either side. Be extremely careful in windy conditions.
- The hut is 10 minutes past the lighthouse near the foot of the hill.

POINTS OF INTEREST

- This is a coastal walk on a grand scale with spectacular views. On the seaward side the pounding surf rides up the sheer cliffs in endless shows of foam. The more sheltered western side has quintessential Bay of Islands views with innumerable headlands, forest-capped islets and tranquil bays at the edge of the clear blue waters.
- The electric fence was constructed in 1995 and crosses the entire width of the peninsula. It was erected to reduce the impact of possum browsing on the coastal vegetation.
- The Cape Brett lighthouse stands 149 m above seal level and was erected in 1909 to help prevent the frequent shipwrecks that were occurring on the New Zealand coastline. A landing block and crane

were constructed to unload the building materials, which were transferred to a tramline, powered by a whim. The route of the lines is still evident today.

- The cast-iron sections were made in a Thames foundry and bolted together on site. The lighting apparatus was the first in New Zealand to revolve in a mercury bath, which reduced the friction.
- Three identical houses were built for the lighthouse keepers and their families. The families ensured the light functioned properly, maintained the buildings, kept stock and communicated with passing vessels.
- In 1941 a military signal station was established to interrogate passing ships. With the threat of a Japanese invasion in 1942, a radar station was built. The remains of many of the structures are dotted around the hillside and make interesting exploring.

39 Whangamumu Track

GRADE 2

TIME 2½ hours return

ACCESS From Russell, follow Russell Road and then turn left into Kempthorne Road towards Rawhiti. This runs into Manawaora Road. At the junction with Rawhiti Road, turn left and the start of the track is signposted after 1 km.

For a small fee, the adjoining property will provide safe parking.

TRACK NOTES

- For 15 minutes, the track crosses sometimes-muddy farmland and is marked with green and yellow posts. It then becomes wide and well formed, but sometimes slippery, as it climbs the hill to the lookout by the junction with the link to the Cape Brett Track.
- Entering the Whangamumu Scenic Reserve, the sometimes-slippery track descends for 20 minutes to the beach.
- The whaling station is a further 5 minutes over the small promontory to the left.

POINTS OF INTEREST

- Whangamumu Harbour is a deep, sheltered cove with a bronze sandy beach and shady pohutukawa.
- From the 1890s to 1940, a whaling station was established on its northern shore. The Cook family were the main instigators and had a

long history of whaling in the family. Some of the children had been born at sea on whaling trips.

- Humpback whales on their known migration past Cape Brett were caught with buoyed nets, anchored by a strong cable to nearby rocks, one now known as Net Rock. When entangled, they were hindered in their movement and easily harpooned. This was the only place in the world where whales were caught by netting and the method was patented. Once ashore, they were cut up, put on wagons and boiled for 36 hours in try pots, the concrete foundation of which are still evident.
- In 1927, at the peak of the station's output, 74 whales were caught, yielding 388 tonnes of oil and 70 tonnes of bone dust. Following the sinking of the tanker *Niagara* in 1940, the oil slick changed the whale's migration path, forcing the closure of the station.
- Most of the men employed came from Rawhiti, and many of their descendants still live in the area.

40 Kauri Grove Walk

GRADE 2
TIME 20 minutes return
ACCESS The start of the walk is signposted from the side of the narrow, winding, unsealed Russell Road, 9 km from the junction with Rawhiti Road near Ngaiotonga, and 2 km from the junction with Kempthorne Road on the Russell side.
TRACK NOTES The track is mostly even and partly metalled. A few short sections involve negotiating tree roots and sharp inclines.
POINTS OF INTEREST Information panels are posted by many trees, including the solid youthful kauri.

Whangaruru

41 Ocean Beach Loop

GRADE 3
TIME 1¾ hours return

ACCESS In Ngaiotonga, turn into Whangaruru North Road and follow it 11 km to the gate. Drop down the hill to the campground at Puriri Bay, where there is parking for walkers. The track starts at the top of the hill south of the Puriri Bay campground.

Toilets are open only during the summer camping season.

TRACK NOTES

- The track is marked occasionally with orange triangles and signposted.
- Walk up the access road to the north of the campground and follow the sometimes-muddy grass track for 15 minutes. The track enters

Active coastal erosion takes place with a display of aquatic fireworks near Ocean Beach at Whangaruru North Head.

forest and after 15 minutes a signpost shows options to head left to Bland Bay Lookout or right to Ocean Beach.

- Head right, and for 30 minutes follow the track along the cliff top, mostly through low manuka, then descend to Ocean Beach.
- Head inland for 15 minutes to the signposted detour (5 minutes return) to the trig, then drop down the hill to Admirals Bay and the ranger's house (10 minutes). It is a further 15 minutes over a farmland track to the top of the hill, south of Puriri Bay.

POINTS OF INTEREST

- Whangaruru North Head is composed of greywacke and rises to nearly 200 m. The open coast is exposed to the sea and rises spectacularly in a series of ridges, dissected by swampy narrow valleys. At the outfall of each stream is a small sandy beach, of which Ocean Beach is the most spectacular, flanked on all sides by high, steep cliffs. The views from the trig look out over Whangaruru Harbour and down to Mimiwhangata.
- The area was once grazed and some still constitutes farmland. Where the pasture has reverted to forest, manuka is abundant. However, over 350 species have been recorded growing on the varied terrain within the reserve.
- Whangaruru means 'sheltered harbour' and was inhabited by hapu of Ngapuhi. At the end of the 1800s nearly 2000 Maori lived in the area and, following the discovery of kauri gum, many worked to excavate the low-lying swamps.

42 Bland Bay Lookout Track

GRADE 3
TIME 1½ hours return
ACCESS As for Ocean Beach Loop.
TRACK NOTES

- The track is marked with occasional orange triangles.
- For 15 minutes the track climbs through sometimes-muddy paddocks and then enters the forest for 15 minutes. At the signpost, bear left and follow the ridge top for 20 minutes to the signpost to the lookout (1 minute return).
- After 10 minutes there is a grass clearing with a lookout to Bland Bay. The track then drops for 20 minutes to a wetland, which is watery underfoot (10 minutes). The track reaches the road 200 m before the

gate at the park entrance. It takes approximately 10 minutes to walk along the road back to Puriri Bay.

- The two walks can be combined to form a 2½-hour loop. It is probably best to start the loop before the park entrance. Look for the solitary orange triangle opposite the power pole at the northern end of the wetland.

POINTS OF INTEREST

- From the lookout to Bland Bay you can see that Whangaruru North Head is joined to the mainland by a tombolo, or sandspit, at Bland Bay. This has enclosed and formed Whangaruru Harbour.
- Bland Bay was the main settlement of Whangaruru and was named in the late 1800s. Two pa flank the low sandy neck. Tewhau was sited on the northern side of Whangaruru Head.

43 Mimiwhangata Coastal Park

Mimiwhangata Coastal Park forms an arcing peninsula that drops from forest-covered hills to a low spine, terminating in a bulbous headland. Many rock islands, known as the Wide Berth Islands, are scattered out to sea.

The eastern side is ringed by Okupe Beach, which is punctuated with small promontories capped in tufts of vegetation, offshore stacks and reefs. The eastern side on Mimiwhangata Bay is more sheltered and enclosed. There are no formal walking tracks in the park, however public access is available to most areas. Through the network of farm tracks, you can

The views from the lookouts at Mimiwhangata encompass the coast and arcing peninsula.

discover the headlands, forests, beaches, rocky promontories, wetlands and farmland.

You will need a sense of direction and a full day to thoroughly explore the diverse landscapes. As there are no marked tracks it is difficult to follow a described route. For this reason any notes on tracks provided here would be confusing.

ACCESS Mimiwhangata is 7 km along Mimiwhangata Road. Turn off Old Russell Road at Helena Bay. The park is signposted along a narrow, winding and unsealed road. At the road-end are toilets.

POINTS OF INTEREST

- Mimiwhangata was the site of fierce battles between the local Ngati Manaia tribe and Ngapuhi, culminating in the Battle of Mimiwhangata at Kaituna. Te Waero, a Ngapuhi chief, was married to two women of rank of Ngati Manaia tribe and had destroyed a fishing net belonging to Ngati Manaia. He was killed for this unforgivable sin, which sparked the battle and a decisive victory for Ngapuhi.
- Te Rearea, Taraputa and Kaituna pa housed the local population, which in pre-European times would have numbered nearly 2000.
- In 1962 the New Zealand Breweries Limited bought the land inending tof construct a massive tourist resort. This caused much resentment among locals and environmentalists, and in 1975 the Mimiwhangata Farm Park Trust was established. The freedom of the public to wander the hills, beaches and forests of its boundaries is still available today.

Kawakawa

44 Ruapekapeka Pa Historic Reserve

GRADE 1

TIME 20 minutes return

ACCESS Ruapekapeka Road is signposted 1 km north of Towai on SH 1, 16 km south of Kawakawa. It is a further 5 km along the unsealed road to a parking area, from where the pa site is signposted.

TRACK NOTES

- The track follows a wide grass strip to the grassed area around the remains of the pa.

- There is a 5-minute-return walk to a large puriri, signposted from the top of the pa. This track is narrow and uneven.

POINTS OF INTEREST

- Ruapekapeka pa was the site of the last battle between government forces and Maori in the Battle of the North from December 1845 to January 1846. Maori and the British Government disagreed on the term 'sovereignty' in the Treaty of Waitangi. Maori believed they could still live as they wished, while the British assumed they had control over all facets of life. The Ngapuhi chiefs Kawiti and Hone Heke were the principal opponents to the British contingent. The battle effectively started when Hone Heke cut down the flagpole in Kororareka (Russell).

  Under the leadership of Governor George Grey, troops were transported by boat and on foot to positions nearby. Guns were hauled through swamps and over bush tracks.

  On 27 December around 700 troops marched from Taumarere and came up against the pa's formidable defences. Not only was the pa perched on a high point, but protective trenches, high walls and underground tunnels, to shelter warriors from mortar fire, had also been constructed. Many remains of the former defences are still evident today.

  By 11 January over 1500 troops were assembled and substantial artillery helped the pa to be seized. On the second day of the battle, Sunday, most Maori warriors retreated to the forest behind the pa to hold Christian services. They had wrongly assumed the government forces would cease fighting on the Sabbath.

The defences of Ruapekapeka pa are still strikingly evident.

Walks around Whangarei

45 Whananaki Coastal Walkway

GRADE 3

TIME 2¼ hours one way; 3½ hours one way including detours

ACCESS The start of the track is signposted from the farm gate at McAuslin Road, although there is no parking nearby. The nearest place to park is at Sandy Bay Recreation Reserve at the northern end of Sandy Bay, where there are also toilets. It's approximately 1 km to the start of the track.

At Whananaki South, the walk is signposted from by the footbridge to Whananaki North at the end of Whananaki South Road. There is limited parking.

TRACK NOTES

- From Sandy Bay the track is marked with orange posts. For approximately 1 hour it follows a metalled farm track between sandy bays. Two accessways to beaches are signposted at the start of the walk and after 30 minutes.
- After approximately 1 hour the track becomes grassed before the signposted detour to *Capitaine Bougainville* Monument (45 minutes return). This crosses a worn track through long grass and young pines to the end of the headland.
- Return by the same track and continue north for approximately 45 minutes along a grassed farm track.
- On leaving views of the beach, the track follows the sandy 4WD track behind Whananaki Recreation Reserve and the beach, before arriving at the estuary (20 minutes).
- Bear left behind the baches. The final 50 m involve walking over firm mudflats. One hour either side of high tide this is not possible without getting wet feet. The property owners on the estuary may let you cross the front of their sections if you ask. The only other alternative route is to bear left along the sandy track opposite Whananaki Recreation Reserve, which exits near the road-end of Whananaki South Road.

POINTS OF INTEREST

- The Whananaki coast is a series of pasture-covered spurs dissected by steep-sided gullies. Headlands capped in vegetation form rocky protrusions at the end of the spurs and provide dramatic coastal views. In the gullies, pohutukawa and kauri mix with occasional puriri and kohekohe.

- At the foot of the gullies are a necklace of sandy beaches, which string along between the headlands.
- The *Capitaine Bougainville* was a French freighter wrecked off the Whananaki coast in 1973; 16 lives were lost when a lifeboat capsized.

46 Whale Bay to Matapouri Bay Loop Walk

GRADE 1 (to Whale Bay); 2 (loop walk)
TIME 30 minutes return to Whale Bay; 1½ hours return
ACCESS From Matapouri Bay continue north 1 km to the summit of the hill where Whale Bay Scenic Reserve is signposted from the parking area.
TRACK NOTES

- This walk is administered by Whangarei District Council and is unmarked. It is well formed and signposted.
- The track is metalled to Whale Bay, where there are toilets.
- After climbing out of Whale Bay, follow the signpost along the headland track. The worn grass track runs between the fenceline and cliff top for 15 minutes, passing the trig before bearing right. The track deteriorates and can be muddy for the 15-minute descent to the gravel beach on the opposite side of the headland from Matapouri Bay.
- Walk along Matapouri Bay to the first wooden accessway and follow Morrison Road. Turn right into Ringer Road, where Morrison Recreation Reserve is signposted (15 minutes).
- The 15-minute climb to the carpark above Whale Bay is signposted and follows the fenceline.

POINTS OF INTEREST

- This walk takes in the attractive sandy beaches of Whale Bay and Matapouri Bay and the memorable coastal scenery of the craggy headlands that jut out to meet a frothing sea.
- Matapouri Bay means 'Invisible Place' or 'Hidden Place', testimony to how the encroaching headlands shelter its half circle of sand. Because the western headland hides Matapouri Bay from the open sea, it was once known as Otito, meaning 'a lie'.
- Whale Bay received its European name during the period of early settlement. A group of Maori saw a large floating object and asked Mr Woolley of nearby Woolleys Bay to lend them his telescope. On

sighting the remains of a dead whale, all men of the region in their canoes rowed out and towed it to Whale Bay.

Crowds camped on the beach for three weeks, tolerating the powerful stench. Whenever these people visited the Woolleys for milk, the smell accompanied them. The tailbone was eventually given to the Woolleys as a gift, which they used as a fire screen.

47 Pukenui Forest Track

GRADE 3

TIME 4 hours return

ACCESS From Whangarei follow SH 1 to Kamo and turn left into Three Mile Bush Road. Some 3.7 km further on the right is a small parking bay by Amalin Drive, from where the start of the walk is signposted.

TRACK NOTES

- The track is well formed, marked with orange triangles and involves the crossing of several narrow streams.
- For approximately 15 minutes the track crosses paddocks and stiles over the dry stone walls to the forest boundary. Head right along the fenceline to a signpost where the track branches (15 minutes).
- Following the track in an anticlockwise direction for 1¼ hours arrives at a large kauri. After 1 hour the track drops to a stream and the junction with the Taraire Ridge Track. To complete the loop takes a further 45 minutes.

POINTS OF INTEREST

- There are many characters to the forest on this walk. On the ridges taraire predominate, while solid totara inhabit the slopes. The large kauri is a remnant of the forest that once covered the area before it was logged in the 1920s.
- Fields of paritaniwha line the streamsides in the gullies.

The stone walls on Pukenui Forest Track, which bring a piece of Yorkshire to the walk, are low maintenance and attractive.

- The stone walls, which bring a slice of Yorkshire to the initial stages of the walk, were constructed by the McGregor brothers around the time of the Second World War. The Whangarei region was littered with angular rocks of volcanic origin. When the land was cleared for agriculture, the rocks were collected and tessellated to form the durable and sturdy walls. Some walls in the region date to the 1860s. The walls were built because of their permanence. They need little maintenance and combine function with attractiveness.

48 A.H. Reed Memorial Kauri Park

GRADE 1, or 2 from base of Pukenui Waterfall to upper carpark
TIME 45 minutes return
ACCESS From Whangarei follow Bank Street and Mill Road then turn right into Whareroa Road. The lower carpark is 1.5 km on the left. The middle carpark, with disabled access to the Canopy Walkway, is 150 m further up the hill. The upper carpark, with a lookout at the top of the Pukenui Falls, is a further 300 m.

TRACK NOTES
- The track is administered by Whangarei District Council.
- Apart from the steep section to the top of Pukenui Falls, the track is of an even gradient and the surface is mostly metalled. Frequent signposts mark the network of tracks through the forest.
- From the lower carpark, cross the small footbridge over Waikoromiko Stream and follow the Elizabeth Track alongside the Hatea River.
- Bear left along the McKinnon Track near the junction with the Canopy Walkway to Pukenui Falls. The track becomes steep and uneven to the top of the falls. The upper carpark has a 20-metre walk to a lookout at the top of the falls.
- Return along the McKinnon Track and then follow the Alexander Walk. This takes in the elevated Canopy Walkway, which crosses the Waikoromiko Stream on a wooden walkway. Wheelchair access for the 10-minute loop around the Canopy Walkway is reached from the middle carpark.
- Return to the lower carpark via the Alexander Walk.

POINTS OF INTEREST
- The magnificent Canopy Walkway gives a rare view of the forest canopy. Rata and kiekie clamber up the tree fern caudices and you can look down onto the burst of nikau fronds below.

- Some youthful kauri are scant reminder of the forest that once clothed the region. With the crashing of the 24-metre high Pukenui Falls nearby and the fresh smells of the forest, this is a memorable forest excursion.
- The area was first inhabited by Ngati Tu and eventually conquered by Ngapuhi. Many chiefs were buried in the area because of its outstanding natural beauty.
- A.H. Reed was born in London in 1875 and arrived in New Zealand in 1887. His father worked in the Northland gumfields, a profession A.H. Reed later took up. His formative years were spent in Whangarei.

    With little formal education, A.H. Reed taught himself shorthand and after winning a job with an Auckland typewriter business moved to Dunedin. In 1907 the publishing house of A.H. and A.W. Reed was founded. (A.W. Reed was A.H.'s nephew.)

    A.H. Reed wrote many works on New Zealand history and kauri, a tree for which he developed a special fondness.

    W.M. Fraser, a pre-First World War Kauri Bushmen's Association member, proposed the renaming of the Parahaki Scenic Reserve for A.H. Reed. In recognition of the accolade, the sum of £25 per year was allocated from the Reed trust fund to ensure the maintenance and upkeep of the park.

49 Whangarei Falls Scenic Reserve

GRADE 1
TIME 30 minutes return
ACCESS From Whangarei follow Bank Street and Mill Road to Tikipunga and turn right into Kiripaka Road. The falls are signposted 500 m further on the right.

There are toilets and a picnic area by the carpark.

TRACK NOTES

- The track is administered by Whangarei District Council.
- The metalled track snakes from the viewing platforms at the top of the falls, through native forest to a footbridge over the Hatea River at the base of the falls. A climb to the eastern side of the river leads to another viewing platform.
- When the water level is low, a concrete track over the river at the top of the falls is exposed. This enables the loop to be completed. If the

concrete is covered by water then the river level is too high and you must return by the same track.

POINTS OF INTEREST

- The Whangarei Falls are 26 m high and cascade in a frothing maelstrom over a solidified basalt lava flow, thought to be around 2.5 million years old.
- Early residents of Whangarei used to visit the falls for a picnic, a pastime that is still popular today.

The Whangarei Falls have been a popular picnic spot for around a hundred years.

50 Mt Manaia Track

GRADE 3

TIME 2 hours return

ACCESS The start of the track is signposted past the settlement of Whangarei Heads along Whangarei Heads Road. There is a parking area below Mt Manaia Club. The start of the track is signposted a little up the hill and leaves from behind the early settlers memorial.

TRACK NOTES

- The track is marked with orange triangles and is uneven and steep. It takes approximately 45 minutes to the signposted Bluff Lookout. This 2-minute detour takes you to an opening in the forest at the top of an exposed rock face. Take extreme care while admiring the view as the wind can gust ferociously.

- The final ascent to the summit takes approximately 15 minutes. A wooden staircase leads to a flat rock area below the main pinnacles. There is no access to the trig at the summit.
- An alternative route is signposted from the top and drops very steeply, sometimes aided with a steel cable to steady the descent. This takes 45 minutes and arrives at the start of the track.

POINTS OF INTEREST

- According to one Maori legend there were five brothers, Manaia, Maungaraho, Tokatoka, Motowhitiki and Taungatara, who were disillusioned with their lives in Hawaiki. Under cover of darkness they decided to follow the findings of the great explorer Kupe and travel to Aotearoa. At dawn the mighty Atua took away their powers of motion, stranding them in their present resting places.
- Manaia, Maungaraho, Tokatoka, and Motowhitiki all lie in a straight line to Ripiro Beach, where Taungatara, the smallest peak, stands. The songs and legends of Ngapuhi and Ngati Whatua remember this story.
- Another Maori legend accounts for the five peaks on the summit ridge relating to Manaia and his family. The largest peak represents Manaia himself, the smaller pinnacles are his children, while the last figure is his unfaithful wife, turning her head away in shame.

- Mt Manaia is the eroded skeleton of an andesite cone, erupted 22–16 million years ago. The layers of andesitic breccia are visible on the summit ridge and rocks in the matrix are visibly exposed on the sides of the pinnacles.
- Rare plant communities adorn the slopes, with parapara, large leaf milk tree and native angelica being some of the more notable

Mt Manaia has many legends embodied in its jagged peaks.

87

species. The exposed rocky ridge has examples of mountain daisy, native forget-me-not and sprawling pomaderis.

- Much of the plant and birdlife is shared with the Three Kings, Hen and Chickens and Poor Knights Island groups.

51 Smugglers Bay Track

GRADE 3

TIME 2 hours return

ACCESS The parking area is signposted at the southern end of Urquharts Bay, from where the start of the track is signposted.

TRACK NOTES

- For 30 minutes the track crosses poorly drained farmland along Woolshed Bay to an old gun emplacement. The track is marked with orange posts.
- It then crosses long grass with sporadic native vegetation for 20 minutes to the junction with the track to Busby Head. This section is marked with orange triangles.

Smugglers Bay received its name from bootleggers who would stash crates of liquor in the dunes to avoid duty at the port of Whangarei.

- You can bear left and return to the carpark over farmland (marked with orange posts), which takes 30 minutes, or head right.
- The track to the headland pa at Busby Head is narrow but well formed and after 10 minutes passes a signpost on the left to Smugglers Bay. To reach the tip of the headland and return to Smugglers Bay takes 30 minutes. The section to Smugglers Bay includes some very slippery areas over exposed rocks.
- The return to the carpark over farmland completes a loop around the hill and takes 20 minutes.

POINTS OF INTEREST
- Smugglers Bay was named because whisky used to be stashed in the dunes behind the bay to avoid customs duty at the port of Whangarei.
- Three high middens flank the rear of the bay. Surveys of the shell and bone that make up the heaps, and radiocarbon dating of the debris, have established the area was occupied for many centuries and the bountiful resources of the sea were well used.
- The main inhabitants were Ngati Wai and their ancestors Ngati Manaia. The headland pa still shows evidence of hangi pits, storage pits and terraces used for the construction of dwellings.
- The gun emplacement was secretly constructed in 1942 and built to look like a farm building. The siting on the western side of the heads sheltered it from enemy observation. A 6-inch naval gun was mounted on a concrete emplacement but only three shots were ever fired. The buildings of the remote control room and generating shed are still intact.

  On the wall in the remote control room is a painted frieze of the landscape in view from the emplacement, with bearings marked beneath. The scenery is depicted before the construction of the Marsden Point Oil Refinery.

52 Peach Cove Track

GRADE 3

TIME 2½ hours return

ACCESS The carpark is approximately 1 km before Ocean Beach and signposted on the right. Park near the main road as the accessway is a private driveway. The start of the track is signposted a little further up the accessway.

TRACK NOTES

- The track is rough and narrow, but formed and marked with orange triangles.
- For the first 30 minutes the track climbs on a worn grass surface through low manuka scrub to a signpost. Bear right and head through the forest for 10 minutes to another signpost at the junction with the Bream Head Track on the ridge. Pass through the electric fence and after 10 minutes Peach Cove is signposted down the south-facing hill.
- For 20 minutes the track drops steeply to Peach Cove Hut. This can be booked at DoC in Whangarei. There is a toilet nearby. Peach Cove is a further 5 minutes.

POINTS OF INTEREST

- Peach Cove is a temporary break in a rocky coastline at the foot of high forest-covered cliffs. The small pebble beach is dominated by the imposing and jagged pinnacles of Bream Head.

53 Bream Head Track

GRADE 4

TIME 5 hours one way

ACCESS To walk the route west to east start from Urquharts Bay carpark at the end of Urquharts Bay Road. Bear left over farmland for 10 minutes to a signpost at the edge of the native forest before the ascent of Mt Lion.

The eastern end can be attempted from Ocean Beach. Follow Ocean Beach Road and turn right into Ranui Road. Continue to the parking area with toilets just before the beach.

The track starts from the southern end of Ocean Beach by climbing the dune.

TRACK NOTES

- The track is marked with orange triangles and is well formed but uneven. It follows the ridge from Mt Lion to Bream Head.
- From Smugglers Bay the track climbs very steeply for 1 hour to the summit of Mt Lion. For the next 1½ hours it descends the ridge to the signposted junction with the Peach Cove Track, passing through a grazed area demarcated with an electric fence. There are occasional clearings with views.

- The climb to the lookout at the summit of Bream Head takes approximately 1¼ hours, although the final mounting of the pinnacles involves clambering up the sheer rock. Take extreme care and if you are wary of heights do not climb the pinnacle. The summit area is very small; be aware of strong wind gusts.
- To reach Ocean Beach, retrace your final few steps from the summit and follow the ridge past the radar station (30 minutes). The final 45 minutes crosses open grassland and is marked with orange posts.

POINTS OF INTEREST

- The views from the summit of Bream Head stretch to the horizon in every direction. You can see the Coromandel Peninsula, Cape Rodney, Hen and Chickens Islands and Whangarei Harbour.
- The peaks of the Bream Head Range are the eroded stumps of former volcanic cones, erupted around 20 million years ago. The volcanic vents were filled with slowly cooling lava, which were more resistant than the layers of ash, pumice, lava and mud forming the surrounding cone. Weathering agents over the millennia have removed the less resistant layers, leaving the exposed neck, known as a volcanic plug. The andesite lava was silica rich and formed dykes such as Taurikura, at the eastern end, and parasitic cones on the main vent.

- With a warm and moist climate, suitable for growing crops, a close proximity to a bountiful sea and a major vantage point, Bream Head would have made a suitable site for Maori occupation. Large midden heaps behind Smugglers Bay indicate populations must have been numerous and inhabited the area for centuries. However, by the time first European contact was made, little evidence of occupation remained.

The ridge to Bream Head provides stunning views where there are gaps in the forest canopy.

Tangihua Forest

The Tangihua Forest covers 3240 ha and rises to 627 m. The predominantly podocarp broadleaf forest is scattered with kauri and occasional hardwood and coastal species.

Between 1911 and 1934 the forest was logged for its kauri and podocarps.

The Tangihua Range is a prominent relief feature of volcanic rock. The steep slopes and jagged hills project boldly from the earlier surrounding rocks. The rock is hard and dark and has been extensively folded and faulted.

The southern access to Tangihua Forest is reached off SH 1, 13 km south of Whangarei along Mangapai Road. After 10.5 km turn right onto Tauraroa Road and after a further 1 km turn left into Omana Road (partly unsealed). Follow it 11.5 km to the signposted carpark on the right.

The Lodge Road is private and continues towards the forest boundary from the carpark. You must park in the designated parking area before the gate. The metalled road takes 30 minutes each way to access the tracks.

54 Kauri Dam Walk

GRADE 2

TIME 1½ hours return from carpark; 30 minutes return from Lodge Road
ACCESS The start of the walk is signposted on the left near a sharp bend in Lodge Road.
TRACK NOTES The track is sporadically marked but well formed. It weaves through forest to a lookout platform above the remains of a dam.
POINTS OF INTEREST

- Kauri dams were used to 'drive' logs from the streambed to booms in the lower reaches of the watersheds for transportation to the mills. During floods the dams would be 'tripped', allowing vast torrents of water to collect the waiting logs. There were various designs for dams depending on their use, but most were sited within steep watersheds, allowing for huge quantities of water to be trapped behind them. All that remains of this dam are the lower beams.

55 Nature Walk

GRADE 2

TIME 1½ hours return from carpark; 30 minutes return from Lodge Road

ACCESS The start of the track is signposted as the Horokaka Track shortly after entering the forest.

TRACK NOTES
- The track climbs through the dense forest over a well-formed and marked track for 15 minutes to a junction. The Nature Walk is signposted to the left and rejoins Lodge Road a little further up from the departure point.

POINTS OF INTEREST
- Information panels by prominent trees explain their ecology and growth habits.
- Watch for the rare kauri snail (*Paryphanta busbyi*), which is a large carnivorous native snail endemic to New Zealand. Its name comes from its shared range with the kauri tree. The shell is approximately 70 mm in diameter and coloured green-brown. Broken shells lie discarded by the trackside, the remains of a substantial meal for native birds.

Waipu and Mangawhai

56 Waipu Caves Walkway

GRADE 3

TIME 2 hours return

ACCESS From SH 1 at Waipu, follow Shoemaker Road and turn left into unsealed Waipu Caves Road. After 500 m veer right into Ormiston Road (unsealed). The start of the track is signposted from a small parking bay 13 km from Waipu.

The caves are reached by continuing 6 km along Waipu Caves Road from the junction with Shoemaker Road. The small parking bay has toilets nearby. The caves are marked at the far side of the paddock, a 2-minute walk from the parking bay.

TRACK NOTES From Ormiston Road, the track is marked with orange posts. Climb the undulating ridge over grass paddocks for 30 minutes. The track enters regenerating podocarp forest (10 minutes) before dropping down a muddy track to the caves.

POINTS OF INTEREST

- The limestone is moderately hard and fine-grained and composed of around 80 percent calcium carbonate. It is a coarse rock, composed of foraminifera (tiny calcareous sea-dwelling creatures) and broken shell fragments, with many recognisable fossils.
- Acid dissolved in percolating groundwater has slowly sculpted the caves, which now form a magnificent cavern, easily accessible near the entrance. Take care around the entrance as the rock can be slippery because water dripping from stalactites leaves a wet film on the surface below.

57 Brynderwyn Walkway

Note: The walkway may sometimes be closed because of logging operations. Check with DoC Whangarei before attempting the walk.

GRADE 4

TIME 6–7 hours one way

ACCESS The walkway is signposted on the eastern side of SH 1 at the summit of Pilbrow Hill opposite the cafe. There is a small parking area. At the eastern end, 5.5 km from Mangawhai Heads on Cove Road towards Waipu, is a small parking area. The start of the track is signposted.

TRACK NOTES

- From Pilbrow Hill, follow the logging road (Artillery Road) for 30 minutes until the signpost on the right.
- Through the regenerating forest the track is rough and undulating, but well marked with orange triangles. There are two small stream crossings.
- After 1 hour the track rejoins a bulldozed road. Frequent slips require careful negotiation. The track is lined with orange marker posts.
- After 1½ hours you reach the junction with Massey Road carpark, which is signposted (45 minutes one way) along a metalled road.
- To continue to Cove Road, follow the metalled forestry road for 45 minutes past a trig to the intersection with other tracks. Follow the private road past houses for 5 minutes and a signpost marks the route into the low kanuka scrub. After 45 minutes you reach another trig, having undulated along an uneven track.

- For 20 minutes the track briefly uses a 4WD track and veers left back into kanuka scrub, exiting at a signal station (25 minutes).
- Shortly after, a signpost indicates the track to the left. This drops steeply through a low canopy with emerging kauri and tanekaha to a stream and paddock near Cove Road (30 minutes).

POINTS OF INTEREST

- The region was originally inhabited by Ngati Whatua. Little archaeological evidence exists of the area's occupation, but the most likely sites would have been near the coast at Mangawhai Heads, in close proximity to the resources of the sea. The best soils occur on the mudstones of Pilbrow Hill and these may also have been likely sites for habitation.
- The Brynderwyn Hills are deeply weathered greywacke rock, with foothills of Tertiary mudstones and sandstones.
- Most vegetation is exotic pine plantations and regenerating manuka scrub. The kauri was logged from the late 1800s to the 1930s.
- The views from the spine of the ridge are extensive in all directions. To the north is the sweep of Bream Bay and to the south Cape Rodney. The outer Hauraki Gulf islands loom large on the horizon. Inland the hazy low hills stretch to the distance and are a patchwork of light green pasture and dark green forest.

58 Mangawhai Cliffs Walkway

Note: The walkway is closed three months of the year for lambing and calving, from 1 July to 30 September.

GRADE 3

TIME 3 hours return

ACCESS From Mangawhai Heads settlement, follow Molesworth Drive north to the roundabout and turn right into Mangawhai Heads Road. Bear left into Wintle Street. The start of the walkway is signposted from the carpark, where there are also toilets.

TRACK NOTES

- Walk along the firm sand of the beach and after 30 minutes the walkway is signposted. The cliff-top section is marked with orange poles. It climbs a steep ridge over farmland before undulating through pockets of coastal forest. After approximately 1 hour it descends to a magnificent rock arch.

- The return along the coast passes over rocks for 30 minutes and is passable only three hours either side of low tide. Otherwise return via the cliff-top route.
- Many small pebbles filter into your boots along the coast, so bring gaiters to avoid having to constantly stop and remove the annoying stones.

POINTS OF INTEREST

- The rocks at the foot of the cliffs range from hexagonally jointed andesite volcanic rocks to rogue boulders of honeycomb-weathered sandstone.
- The track weaves over pebble beaches and extensive promontories filled with rock pools. Black nerita snails speckle the multicoloured rocks and barnacles and mussels inhabit the upper tidal reaches.
- Steep cliffs clothed with stunted manuka and flax have pohutukawa at their bases, in which are rookeries of pied shags. High pingao-covered dunes are near the carpark.

The Mangawhai Cliffs Walkway takes in forest, farmland and coastal scenery.

Walks around Warkworth

59 Dome Forest Walkway

GRADE 3

TIME 1 hour return

ACCESS The walkway is signposted from by the cafe at the top of Dome Hill, 6 km from Warkworth on SH 1 to Wellsford.

TRACK NOTES

- The track steps steadily through native forest to a ridge on a metalled surface. The track along the ridge is well formed but uneven and latticed with tree roots.

POINTS OF INTEREST

- The Dome Lookout faces southeast and looks to Warkworth and the eastern jaw of Mahurangi Harbour. The Dome Forest consists of 401 ha of regenerating podocarp and broadleaf trees, which were logged in the early 1900s.
- A canopy of kauri, rimu, miro, totara, kahikatea, taraire, puriri and kohekohe overtop an understorey of mapou, tree ferns, rangiora and mingimingi.
- The tiny Hochstetter's frog (*Leiopelma hochstetteri*) hides in damp places in the forest. The endemic species is very rare and misses out the tadpole stage in reproduction.
- The Dome is said to be the final resting place of the Tainui ancestor Reipae and her sister Reitu. They flew to Whangarei Harbour on the back of a bird.

Tawharanui Regional Park

Tawharanui Regional Park sits on the tip of a protruding limb of resistant greywacke, which commands spectacular views in all directions.

Compared to the relative intimacy of inner Waitemata Harbour inlets and coves, the views at Tawharanui Regional Park are on a grander scale. The inner Hauraki Gulf islands are replaced with the Moehau Range of the Coromandel Peninsula, Great Barrier Island, Little Barrier Island, Hen and Chickens Islands and Bream Head.

A network of tracks criss-cross the park. Most are either on a metalled surface or over a grass track on pastureland. There are three loop walks through pasture and forest, over craggy coastal rocks and along golden sandy beaches. Access to Tawharanui Regional Park is signposted past Matakana along Takatu Road. There are toilets at Anchor Bay and near the information buildings. Picnic tables and parking are at the lagoon carpark on the entrance road and at Anchor Bay at the road-end.

Take care familiarising yourself with the track layout on the information panels, as it can be complicated to decipher.

The park is administered by Auckland Regional Council.

60 Maori Bay Coast Walk/South Coast Loop Track

GRADE 3

TIME 2¼ hours return

ACCESS The start of the track is signposted from the lagoon carpark.

TRACK NOTES

- Three hours either side of low tide you can follow the coast from Jones Bay to Maori Bay. This takes 1 hour of hopping over coastal boulders, rock shelves and pebble-strewn beaches.
- After approximately 45 minutes look for the large rock that resembles an unfurling elephant trunk. The steep grass track from Maori Bay is just the other side of the next headland.
- The final 1¼ hours weaves through regenerating forest and pastureland along the South Coast Track. This section of the walk is signposted and marked with white-banded posts.

POINTS OF INTEREST

- The rock pools on the coastal section of the walk are interesting to dredge through.
- Views of the northern side of Kawau Island and the Kawau Channel shelter the intimacy of the sinuous coastline around Snells Beach and the eastern arm of Mahurangi Harbour.

61 North Coast Track

GRADE 3
TIME 3½ hours return (including 1½ hours return to Tokatu Point)
ACCESS The start of the track is signposted from Anchor Bay carpark.

TRACK NOTES

- Follow the metalled coast road for 10 minutes and cross the footbridge. The start of the North Coast Track is signposted. This undulates over farmland for 45 minutes past a trig to the junction with the Tokatu Point Track.
- You can spend 1½ hours exploring the headland via Tokatu Loop Track or just 30 minutes walking to the lookout at Tokatu Point.
- An alternative return route via the Fisherman's Track is marked with red-banded posts and cuts through forest. The track is partially metalled.
- You can also return along the Ecology Trail, marked with yellow-banded posts, which provides the best walking surface.
- All return routes lead to Anchor Bay and take approximately 1¼ hours.

POINTS OF INTEREST

- Rare prostrate manuka at Tokatu Point form low clumps. They usually grow as trees, but in these conditions remain low to the ground like shrubs.
- There are magnificent views of the outer Hauraki Gulf islands, which sit like sombre hulks on the horizon. The Hen and Chickens Islands resemble a slumbering crocodile.

62 Westend Track

GRADE 2
TIME 1½ hours return
ACCESS The start of the track is signposted to the west of Anchor Bay carpark.

TRACK NOTES

- The track follows pasture for 15 minutes over a low undulating ridge before bearing left through a cattle yard along a metalled farm track.

- The undulating climb over sometimes-muddy pasture to the Pohutukawa Lookout takes 30 minutes before the track drops to the beach (15 minutes).
- An alternative Shortcut Track is signposted from just after the cattle yard and cuts 15 minutes and the gradient out of the journey to the western end of Anchor Bay.
- Follow the beach around Comets Rocks and Flat Rocks to return to Anchor Bay (30 minutes).

POINTS OF INTEREST

- Little Barrier Island dominates the horizon like a monolith.
- The beaches are all north facing and idyllic spots in which to spend time. A sprinkling of shells decorate the firm, fine, golden sand, and dunefields recede behind.

Kawau Island

63 Kawau Island Tracks

GRADE 2

TIME 2 hours return

ACCESS Ferries leave from Sandspit to Kawau Island. There is also a ferry from Auckland.

TRACK NOTES

- All tracks on Kawau Island pass under a canopy of radiata pines, with a carpet of needles on the forest floor. The tracks are well formed and signposted, but mostly unmetalled.
- From the wharf at Mansion House Bay follow the front fence of Mansion House and climb the headland to Momona Point. The track loops back and follows cliffs along the western coastline to Lady's Bay (30 minutes). After 15 minutes at the grass clearing and lookout, follow the Miners Track for 15 minutes to the old copper mine. At low tide walk across the rocks to the ruins of Coppermine Engine House.
- Past the chimney the track climbs to a grass clearing from where the Redwood Track leads through a shady gully to Two House Bay (45 minutes).
- The 15-minute climb over the steep headland to Mansion House Bay is metalled.

POINTS OF INTEREST

- Ngati Tai lived on the island, fiercely guarding the renowned nearby fishing grounds containing bountiful muru (small spotted shark). They cultivated land around Momona Point (Momona means 'fertile land').

- In the 1830s green stains were noticed on the cliffs near South Cove and this prompted the exploration for copper and manganese. In 1844 both were discovered and for 15 years 400 people were employed in one of New Zealand's earliest industries. Over 3000 tonnes of copper were mined with a value of £60,000. Mining ceased in 1855, but the 70-foot-high brick chimney of the engine house still stands at Dispute Cove.

- In 1862 Sir George Grey bought Kawau Island for £3500 and invested his love of arts and natural history, energy, and a hint of eccentricity into creating a private kingdom. He planted exotic botanical species, brought from his time in Australia and South Africa. He introduced animals such as zebra, Chinese peacock, monkey, antelope, kookaburra and wallaby.

Grey lived at Mansion House from 1870 to 1874 and was premier of New Zealand from 1877 to 1879. He collected around 8000 rare books, which he gifted to Auckland Public Library, and was socially egalitarian, building a school for his employees' children at School House Bay. He sold Kawau Island in 1888 for £12,000 and died in 1898 with £800 to his name.

- Today all these remnants of the island's history form an exotic mix that creates a unique and warm atmosphere to a walk around the island. Although the walks can be accomplished in 2 hours, you are better to spend the day on the island and explore the Mansion House as well.

The chimney from the copper mine is the main relic of the industry on Sir George Grey's exotic paradise.

Other Warkworth walks

64 Tamahunga Summit Trail

GRADE 3

TIME 3 hours return

ACCESS From Leigh, follow Pakiri Road to the top of Pakiri Hill and turn left into Rodney Road. The metalled road follows the ridge to a parking area at the road end. The start of the track is signposted 200 m further on.

TRACK NOTES

- The track forms part of Te Araroa (The long pathway).
- For the first 45 minutes it follows a fenceline over sometimes-muddy and steep farmland. White rings are painted on the fenceposts.
- Entering the forest, the track becomes more poorly formed, but is well marked with orange triangles (45 minutes). The final 15 minutes to the summit becomes steep and involves climbing over rocks.

POINTS OF INTEREST

- Tamahunga (436 m) is the highest point for a considerable distance in all directions. The coastal and landward views are best from the farmland section of the walk or from a lookout 5 minutes before reaching the summit trig.
- The trail was used by Te Kiri, a Ngati Wai chief who liberated Maori prisoners of war from Kawau Island in the 1860s. The trail linked Ngati Wai territories in the north with Ngati Whatua tribal areas in the south.
- Te Hiko o te Kiri (Tamahunga Summit Trail) was opened on 16 December 2001 by Sir Edmund Hillary. The wooden slab at the start of the walk was carved by Neil Devantier as part of Te Araroa celebrations.

65 Mt Auckland Walkway

GRADE 3

TIME 2¾ hours return

ACCESS Mt Auckland Walkway is signposted along Kaipara Hills Road 26 km south of Wellsford along SH 16. Follow the unsealed road 3 km to a large parking bay on the right, from where the start of the walk is signposted.

The elevated viewing platform at the summit of Mt Auckland allows endless views in all directions.

TRACK NOTES

- The track traverses farmland for 25 minutes. Bear left at the top of the farm track and follow the ridge over a low saddle before entering native forest in the Atuanui Conservation Area.
- The track is then marked with orange triangles and is well formed with occasional muddy spots. The 1-hour climb to the summit passes two signposted detours (both less than 5-minutes return) to kauri trees. The climb is gentle but steady and reaches a lookout platform by a trig on the 305 m summit.

POINTS OF INTEREST

- The extensive views of Kaipara Harbour are reserved for gaps in the vegetation before the summit. On a clear day you can see Bream Head, Hen and Chickens Islands, Little Barrier and Great Barrier islands, the Moehau Range of the Coromandel and everything in between.
- The defensive ditch and middens near the summit indicate the presence of a Maori pa.

Greater
Auckland

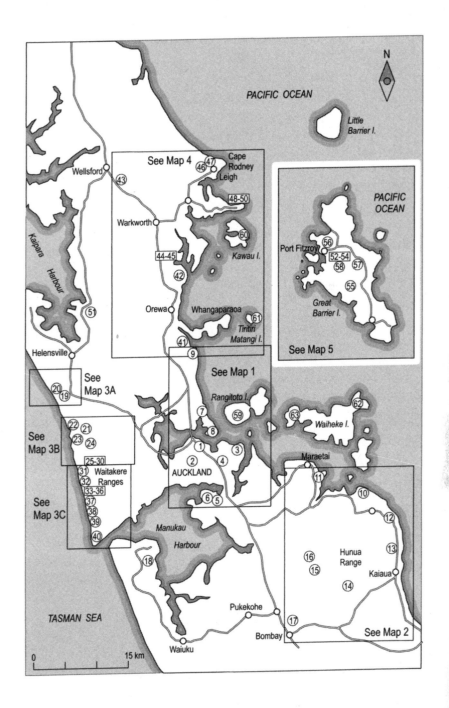

Introduction

Aucklanders are fortunate to have access to an incredibly wide range of landscapes, both in the urban area and the surrounding country. This book covers the Greater Auckland area from Goat Island in the north to the Hunua Ranges in the south. The majority of the walks are within an hour's drive of downtown Auckland. For convenience it is has been divided into five areas, each with its own distinctive flavours.

City
The walks in Auckland have been selected because they offer some unique natural features. All are easy walks that require no special preparation.

South
In the south are the rugged Hunua Ranges and, in marked contrast, the gentle bays and beaches of the Firth of Thames coast.

West
For the more adventurous, the area to the west of the city can be rough and wild, and the walker should be every bit as prepared as if they were going on a back-country tramp. However, within this area are gentler walks on well-formed and well-marked tracks, suitable for all the family.

North
The northern region is an area of bays and beaches, most of which look out to the Hauraki Gulf. These walks are generally short and are best combined with picnics and swimming.

Islands
Islands have always had a special appeal, and the 40 islands in the Hauraki Gulf offer a wide variety of walks of all lengths and levels of difficulty. Great Barrier Island is the only island that will take more than a day to visit.

Top 12 walks
The following trips are the top 12 recommended walks in the Auckland area (one for each month of the year). They will give the walker a good introduction to a variety of landscapes in the area.

Karekare Beach.

Auckland Coast to Coast Walkway (4 hours one way)
An excellent way to grasp the essence of Auckland city, starting from the centre and taking in two of Auckland's most famous volcanic cones, Mount Eden (Maungawhau) and One Tree Hill (Maungakiekie), as well as historic Albert Park and the Domain.

Tahuna Torea Nature Reserve (1 hour)
An attractive mix of coastal vegetation and tidal sandspit, home to shore birds and migrant wading birds. Dead flat and an ideal place to spend two or three hours on a sunny afternoon.

Tawhitokino Bay Walk (1½ hours return)
A beautiful isolated bay fringed with pohutukawa, good for swimming at all tides.

Hunua Falls/Cosseys Reservoir Walk (3 hours loop track)
Beginning at the picturesque Hunua Falls, this walk takes in the reservoir and Cosseys Creek Gorge.

Cascade Kauri, Auckland City Walk, Waitakere Ranges Regional Park (1 hour return) An easy walk on a well formed track with beautiful native bush lining the Waitakere Stream. The highlight is two magnificent kauri that somehow escaped the loggers.

Mercer Bay Loop Walk (1½ hours)
Magnificent coastal scenery from Te Ahua Point with huge cliffs dropping into a wild sea. The track is well formed and marked.

Whatipu–Gibbons Track (6 hours return)
For the more adventurous, this trip combines great coastal scenery with a taste of wild New Zealand, especially with a strong southwesterly blowing.

Okura Bush Walkway (4 hours return to Dacre Cottage)
This walk begins through a magnificent grove of puriri, skirts the Okura River and ends up at historic Dacre Cottage, combining the best of bush, sea and history.

Tawharanui Regional Park
A number of walks criss-cross the park, so you can make them as short or as long as you like. The walking is easy and open with unrestricted views out to Little Barrier Island and the Hauraki Gulf. Anchor Bay is one of the most beautiful beaches in the area.

Rangitoto Island (allow at least half a day)
Just 30 minutes from downtown Auckland, Rangitoto is Auckland's youngest island at a mere 600 years old. A combination of superb views, unique volcanic landscape and unusual plant life makes this a trip hard to beat.

Kawau Island (allow a full day)
Although the walks are no longer than two hours, the historic Mansion House and the derelict copper mine make this an island well worth visiting.

Tiritiri Matangi Island (allow a full day)
An opportunity to see some of this country's rarest birds, such as saddleback and takahe. The native bush on this island reserve has been replanted by thousands of volunteers over the past 30 years. Good walking tracks, a historic lighthouse and Gulf views make for a satisfying day out.

Safety when walking in Greater Auckland

- It can rain with unabated ferocity any time of the year in Greater Auckland. If it has been raining before or during your walk, streams may be at flood level. Make sure the water level is safe to cross. Do not attempt to cross a stream in flood — wait until it subsides. Check tide times for tidal walks along the coast before starting out.

- Always check the weather forecast before departing. Weather can change very quickly.

- Always take enough water, food, sunblock, warm clothes and, if necessary, shelter for your walk. Make sure you are fit enough for the grade of walk you are attempting.

- Possum trappers use many tracks through the forest. Their routes and bait traps are marked with *pink* triangles. Do not follow these. Follow *orange* triangles only. Other common track markers include orange rectangles (which look like pieces of Venetian blinds) and orange posts. Take care as markers can sometimes be sporadic. If in doubt return to your last known point and proceed.

- Inform a friend, relative or Department of Conservation (DoC) Visitor Centre of your intended itinerary before departing on walks into backcountry areas.

Windy Canyon, Great Barrier Island.

○ Take a detailed map and compass. These will not only aid navigation but also inform you of interesting features in the area. NZ 260 Map Series 1:50,000 are useful.

○ Many walks pass through concealed valleys and remote coastal areas. Cellphone repeater stations are scarce. Do not rely on cellphones as safety devices, even on the summits of hills.

○ Although many of these walks are in semiurban areas, some of the tracks are every bit as rugged as backcountry tracks. A surprising number of people have been lost in the Waitakere Ranges. Dense bush can conceal steep cliffs and rocky bluffs, and cliffs along the coast are often unstable and prone to erosion.

Track grades

Please note that these grades are subjective and are provided as a guide only. Tracks are graded according to length, gradient and surface.

1 Track surface is metalled or even with only minor undulations. Directions are clearly signposted. Walks usually take less than an hour.

2 Track may be metalled or unmetalled. It is clearly marked and well formed but usually involves some inclines.

3 Track is unmetalled but well formed and usually marked. Can be uneven and boggy with frequent inclines.

4 Track is usually formed but may be marked or unmarked. It may be very steep, uneven or boggy. These walks are usually reserved for people of good fitness with some outdoor experience.

For walks graded 2 and above, you should be adequately prepared with food and water. It is advisable to wear strong shoes, preferably sturdy boots, and take a detailed map (for example, NZ 260 Map Series 1:50,000 Topomap). Tracks in the Auckland area are often very muddy and slippery, even in summer.

Where a track can be attempted from both directions, the descriptions given in the book apply to one direction only. If you attempt a walk in one direction only, make sure you arrange suitable transport to meet you at the walk's conclusion.

Marked tracks usually have orange triangles or strips nailed to trees. Each marker is usually visible from the previous one, but marking can sometimes be sporadic. If you think you have strayed from the track, retrace your steps to the last reference marker. Do not follow pink, blue or yellow triangles — they are there to guide possum trappers and managers of bait stations and droplines.

Walks through areas administered by Auckland City Council are usually marked with colour-coded posts. These are generally reliable, however where tracks fork or are joined by side-tracks, the system can become confusing. Study information panels at most carparks for details, or contact the Council for further information.

New Zealand Environmental Care Code

When walking in Greater Auckland, follow the Environmental Care Code.

- Protect rare and endangered plants and animals.
- Remove rubbish. Take it away with you.
- Bury toilet waste in a shallow hole away from waterways, tracks, campsites and huts.
- Keep streams clean.
- Take care with fires. If you must build a fire, keep it small, use dead wood, and douse it with water when you leave. Before you go, remove any evidence. Portable stoves are preferable, as they are more efficient and pose less risk to the environment.
- After camping, leave the site as you found it.
- Keep to the track. This minimises the chances of treading on fragile seedlings and root systems.
- Respect the cultural heritage.
- Enjoy yourself.
- Consider others. Respect everybody's reasons for wanting to enjoy Greater Auckland's beauty.

Birds of Greater Auckland

The songs of native birds can be conspicuously absent from the Greater Auckland forests. An eerie quietness often presides over the forest

Sheep at Stoney Batter Walkway, Waiheke Island.

interior. Introduced predators and habitat clearance have kept populations low and the forests devoid of their most tuneful residents.

Occasionally your attention may be caught by the sudden appearance of a fantail, perched on a nearby branch. The whistling sound of a New Zealand pigeon's wings may attract your attention skywards. Perhaps the dulcet calls of a tui or bellbird may even cause you to stop and search the canopy in an attempt to catch a glimpse of the musical genius. But these encounters occur with unfortunate rarity. With the introduction of humans, and especially the Pakeha, came mammalian predators. Rats, mice and feral cats climb trunks and negotiate the branches to feed on eggs and chicks. Stoats, ferrets and weasels are attracted to nestlings, and prey on the defenceless chicks while the parents are away feeding.

Vast tracts of forest have been cleared for agricultural purposes. The diminished habitat has resulted in declining populations of many New Zealand birds including the kiwi, kaka and kokako as well as the more common species such as tui and New Zealand pigeon.

On the coast, the habitat and breeding areas of terns, oystercatchers and dotterels have been decimated by building and competitive land uses. Shallow, exposed nests fall prey to feral cats, domestic dogs and vehicles. Some species such as the New Zealand dotterel are now very rare.

Predator control programmes implemented by DoC and ARC are aimed at reversing this decline and are meeting with some success. Fencing off coastal breeding grounds and increasing public awareness allow populations to recover. Where warning signs are posted, heed their advice and keep away, especially during the spring and summer breeding seasons.

These are some forest residents you will meet.

Fantail (*Rhipidura fuliginosa*)

The friendly fantail will greet you with an energetic 'cheep' as you walk along or pause to rest. Performing aerial acrobatics between perches and displaying its livery on alighting, the fantail will always succeed in attracting your attention. Fantails will often follow you, preying on the insects disturbed as you pass.

The fantail feeds from dawn to dusk, executing skilful movements in midair to catch flying insects. Males will show off to visitors by dropping their wings and fanning their tails.

Tui (*Prosthemadera novaeseelandiae*)

The melodic tones of the tui often penetrate the forest interior. Singing from dawn to dusk, these virtuoso musicians have a formidable repertoire of pure bell-like notes.

Distinguished by its white throat patch, the tui is an important member of the forest community. By eating nectar and fruit and often travelling large distances to abundant food sources, the tui helps disperse seeds and pollinate plants.

New Zealand pigeon
(*Hemiphaga novaeseelandiae*)

The herbivorous New Zealand pigeon, or kereru (also known as kukupu and kuku), will be seen either feeding voraciously on a variety of native fruits or resting on a sunny perch digesting its meal. It will give itself away by causing berries to drop from the canopy while gorging on a feast of fruit.

Its preferred diet is composed of the larger-fruited podocarps such as miro and matai. Species such as tawa, taraire and karaka rely heavily on the kereru for seed dispersal. Because of its wide gape, the kereru can eat large fruit. Little abrasion of the seed occurs in the gizzard, allowing seeds to pass through the digestive system intact. In this way the kereru ensures the perpetuation of its food source.

On the coast look for these birds.

New Zealand dotterel (*Charadrius obscurus*)

The shy and reserved cheeps of the New Zealand dotterel accompany a walk along many Northland beaches. Pairs are loyal and usually stay within sight of each other. They step lightly like ballerinas over the sand and keep a safe distance from humans. They may fake a broken wing to discourage you from passing too close to nests.

Dotterels lay camouflaged eggs in shallow hollows in the dunes and their nests are prone to disturbance. Keep dogs under control and keep out of fenced areas during the breeding season.

Variable oystercatcher (*Haematopus unicolor*)

These birds, which show plumage colour variations from pied to black, are normally seen in pairs and kick up a vociferous racket when approached. Their whistling cheeps are projected at the slightest chance of intrusion. They will often walk a considerable distance up the beach before taking flight.

They fly low to the water with a powerful wing-flap and feed at the mouth of rivers and estuaries. Often their footprints can be traced to encircle a bivalve, whose shells they prise open with their long red bills.

Caspian tern (*Sterna caspia*)

Distinguished from the more boisterous red-billed gull by its pointed wings and a more erratic wing-flap, Caspian terns are expert divers. Deftly spying fish by hovering above the water, they can dive with expert aerobatic skills to capture their prey.

Their red bill and black face-markings contrast with their grey back and white underparts. They will often be seen in flocks resting on offshore stacks or coastal rocky outcrops.

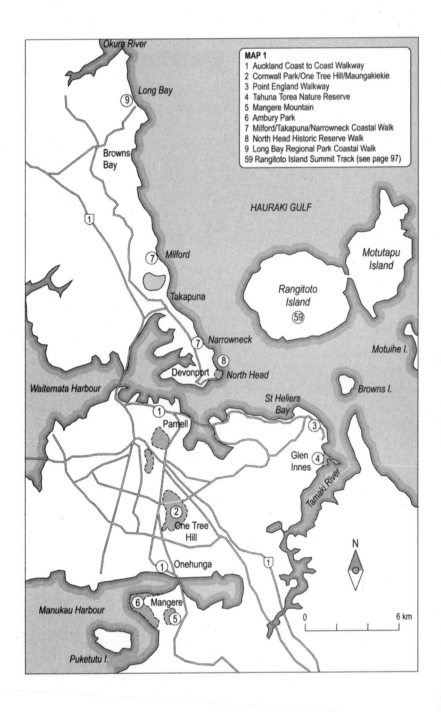

MAP 1
1 Auckland Coast to Coast Walkway
2 Cornwall Park/One Tree Hill/Maungakiekie
3 Point England Walkway
4 Tahuna Torea Nature Reserve
5 Mangere Mountain
6 Ambury Park
7 Milford/Takapuna/Narrowneck Coastal Walk
8 North Head Historic Reserve Walk
9 Long Bay Regional Park Coastal Walk
59 Rangitoto Island Summit Track (see page 97)

Okura River

Long Bay

⑨

Browns
Bay

①

HAURAKI GULF

Motutapu
Island

Rangitoto
Island
㊿

⑦ Milford

Takapuna

Motuihe I.

⑦ Narrowneck

⑧

Devonport North Head

Waitemata Harbour

Browns I.

St Heliers
Bay

①
Parnell

③

Glen
Innes ④

Tamaki River

②
One Tree
Hill

N

① Onehunga

①

⑥ Mangere
⑤

Manukau Harbour

0   6 km

Puketutu I.

CITY WALKS

Sitting between two magnificent harbours, Auckland City is spoilt for choice when it comes to walks. The majority of the walks are very short and are easy to find and follow. A good city street map will have them marked or your local council will have details.

The walks included in this book are ones that require a certain degree of fitness and are reasonably long (over one hour). They take in Auckland's most notable geographical features, its long and varied coastline and its volcanic origin.

Two highly recommended walks are:

Auckland Coast to Coast Walkway (4 hours one way)
An excellent way to grasp the essence of Auckland City, starting from the CBD and taking in two of Auckland's most famous volcanic cones, Mt Eden (Maungawhau) and One Tree Hill (Maungakiekie), as well as historic Albert Park, the Domain and lesser known parks and reserves.

Tahuna Torea Nature Reserve (1 hour)
This walk lets you see an attractive mix of coastal vegetation and tidal sandspit and is home to shore and migrant wading birds. Dead flat walking, it is an ideal place to spend two or three hours on a sunny afternoon.

Tahuna Torea Nature Reserve. Peter Janssen

1 Auckland Coast to Coast Walkway

GRADE 2

TIME 4 hours

ACCESS The walk starts in Queen Elizabeth II Square at the bottom of Queen Street in central Auckland and finishes at Beachcroft Avenue, Onehunga.

TRACK NOTES
- An urban walk of 13 km including well-known Auckland landmarks such as the Domain, Mount Eden, and One Tree Hill.
- A regular bus service from the bus terminal in Onehunga will take you back to the start.
- Although the walk is well signposted, a street map of Auckland will come in very handy.

POINTS OF INTEREST
- Recommended for visitors and locals alike, this walk links some of Auckland's most prominent landmarks, but also includes a number of lesser known parks and reserves such as the University of Auckland gardens. The walk is a great opportunity to see the city on foot rather than from a car.
- Historic Onehunga has an excellent example of a Carnegie library. It also has a number of good cafés so, for a pleasant change, this is one walk you can enjoy without a pack.

2 Cornwall Park/One Tree Hill/Maungakiekie

GRADE 1

TIME 2 hours

ACCESS The beginning of the walk is just inside the Greenlane entrance to the park. The track is not obvious, but starts at the stile at the end of the stone wall on the left of the entrance gateway. The track finishes across the drive, to the right of the gates.

TRACK NOTES
- The track follows the perimeter of the park and crosses open paddocks for the most part. If you wish to climb to the top the best point to do this is on the western side of the park where the road goes.

POINTS OF INTEREST

○ Arguably Auckland's most famous volcanic cone, One Tree Hill or Maungakiekie, has several clearly defined craters, the most obvious of which is on the western side of the summit. The view from the top — the best in Auckland — gives a visitor immediate access to the geography of Auckland with the Waitemata Harbour and Hauraki Gulf to the north, and Manukau Harbour to the south and west.

○ The pa site remains are extensive and easily visible and it is not hard to imagine what the area looked like in pre-European times.

○ The park has several tree plantings of significance, including avenues of oaks and pohutukawa, stands of rimu and kauri, and a grove of mature olive trees above a picturesque Cornwall Park Cricket Ground.

○ The historic Acacia Cottage and the information kiosk in the middle of the park by the café and toilets are both worth a visit and are free of charge.

○ Part of the park is a working farm and the cattle and sheep are very used to visitors. Dogs must be kept on a leash.

○ Attractive old volcanic rock walls are a feature of the park.

○ The name 'One Tree Hill' has a long and intriguing history. In early times the hill was dominated by a sacred totara tree, which was cut down by a Pakeha in the nineteenth century. This tree was replaced with a radiata pine, which in turn was twice attacked by Maori activists, and later removed by the council. New trees have been planted to replace the pine.

3 Point England Walkway

GRADE 2

TIME 4–5 hours

ACCESS This walk begins at the Achilles Point lookout at the top of Cliff Road, St Heliers, above Ladies Bay.

TRACK NOTES

○ The walkway begins at Achilles Point and finishes at the Apirana Reserve on St Johns Road, taking in a number of parks and reserves along the way, including Churchill Park, Tahuna Torea Reserve and Point England Reserve.

- From Apirana Reserve back to Achilles Point is about a 45-minute walk.
- A street map of Auckland is helpful as the track is at points badly signposted.

POINTS OF INTEREST
- The walk features viewpoints out to the north and east overlooking the Hauraki Gulf and Tamaki River. The highlight is the Tahuna Torea Nature Reserve, which includes a long sandspit that at low tide reaches far out into the Tamaki estuary (see next entry).

- The section from Point England to Apirana Reserve is poorly signposted and the path badly formed.

4 Tahuna Torea Nature Reserve

GRADE 1

TIME 1 hour

ACCESS The walk begins at the carpark at the end of West Tamaki Road.

TRACK NOTES
- Easy walking on a well-marked track through coastal vegetation and then on to the sandspit jutting out into the Tamaki estuary.

- An ideal walk for all age groups.

Tahuna Torea Nature Reserve.   Peter Janssen

POINTS OF INTEREST

- The area near the carpark is a mixture of tidal creeks, mudflats and coastal vegetation, and is home to a wide range of wildlife including ducks and pukeko. The area is a summer feeding ground for many migrant wading birds.

- A special feature of the walk is a narrow sandspit that at low tide juts far out into the estuary, taking you about three-quarters of the way across the Tamaki River.

5 Mangere Mountain

GRADE 1

TIME 1 hour

ACCESS The walk begins at the carpark of the Onehunga and Mangere Central Soccer Club in the Mangere Domain at the end of Domain Road, which is off Coronation Road, Mangere Bridge.

TRACK NOTES

- Although the walk is not clearly marked, it is impossible to get lost. Follow the worn path along the crater rim, which will eventually lead you back to the carpark.

POINTS OF INTEREST

- Mangere is Auckland's largest volcano and covers a surprisingly wide area. Less crowded than other parks, it is ideal for a quiet walk and can be combined with a visit to nearby Ambury Park (see next entry).

- As for other volcanic cones around Auckland, traces of Maori occupation, especially terracing and feed storage pits, are clearly visible.

- Excellent views out to the west across Manukau Harbour.

6 Ambury Park

GRADE 1

TIME 1 hour

ACCESS The walk starts at the park headquarters on Ambury Road, Mangere Bridge.

TRACK NOTES

○ A flat well-marked walk suitable for all ages through the farm and then around the tidal shoreline back to the carpark.

○ Ideal combined with Mangere Mountain for a good day out.

POINTS OF INTEREST

○ This park has extensive information boards along the length of the walk, detailing both the natural and human history of the area.

○ The area is also an important feeding ground for migrant wading birds.

○ Like Cornwall Park, it is also used as a farm, and the farm animals will appeal to the very young.

7 Milford/Takapuna/Narrowneck Coastal Walk

GRADE 2

TIME 1¼ hours return from Milford to Takapuna; 3 hours return from Milford to Narrowneck.

ACCESS At the Milford end the walk starts at Milford Reserve off Craig Road; or start at the other end from Narrowneck Beach.

TRACK NOTES

○ From Milford Reserve follow the beach until you reach the pathway that takes you around to Takapuna Beach. From Takapuna Beach follow the shoreline around to Narrowneck. There are some rocky stretches between Milford and Takapuna that will require a modest degree of fitness.

○ You will need to keep a close eye on the tide as access is impossible at high tide between Takapuna and Narrowneck, and even between Milford and Takapuna you will get your feet wet at high tide, especially in rougher weather. An alternative is to walk back along the road if the tide is tricky.

POINTS OF INTEREST

○ This is a very pleasant walk in all seasons and weathers. Wide views over the Hauraki Gulf are combined with close-up views of some of Auckland's more interesting real estate. Multimillion-dollar homes sit alongside the occasional old bach, left over from when this area was a holiday retreat from Auckland.

○ The lava flows at Milford are a graphic reminder of Auckland's very recent volcanic past. At the boat ramp at the north end of Takapuna Beach a feature is the large number of holes in the lava. These were formed by lava flowing around trees that have long since disappeared, leaving only their outlines in the rock.

○ At Thorne's Beach, between Milford and Takapuna, water gushes out between the lava rocks. This is fresh water, believed to be from Lake Pupuke, which has no other visible outlet.

○ Milford, Takapuna and Narrowneck beaches are good swimming at all tides, and the pie shop at Narrowneck serves tasty pies, ice cream and coffee.

8 North Head Historic Reserve Walk

GRADE 1

TIME 1 hour return

ACCESS From Devonport Wharf, follow King Edward Parade east to Torpedo Bay and turn left into Cheltenham Road. Takarunga Road on the right leads up the hill to the parking areas. There are toilets at the southern end of the summit buildings.

TRACK NOTES

○ The track is marked from the lower carpark with white arrows on green posts, which lead through most of the points of interest on the walk.

○ The grassed track on the hill summit area is sometimes difficult to follow, but it is very difficult to get lost.

○ The coastal section of the walks starts from the southwestern corner of the reserve. Pass through the tunnel (a torch is handy but not necessary) and follow the rocky coastline to below the carpark.

POINTS OF INTEREST

○ One of the best views of Auckland is from North Head, with wide views east out over the Hauraki Gulf, south to the city and eastern shoreline, west to Devonport and the upper harbour and north over North Shore. Large crowds are drawn to this vantage point when major events are held on the harbour, but on any sunny day this is a great spot to watch the world go by.

At the end of the nineteenth century, defences were constructed on North Head to protect Auckland City in response to fears of a Russian invasion. They were extended during both world wars.

- Like so many vantage points in Auckland, North Head is an extinct volcano, as is nearby Mount Victoria (above Devonport village).

- Cheltenham Beach is a particularly safe beach for swimming, especially at high tide.

- There are extensive remains, both above and below ground, of the gun emplacements set up to protect the city and coastline. A torch is necessary to explore these thoroughly.

9 Long Bay Regional Park Coastal Walk

GRADE 2

TIME $2^{3}/_{4}$ hours return

ACCESS Long Bay Regional Park is reached by turning into Glenvar Road from East Coast Road and following it through Long Bay until you come to Beach Road. The park entrance is on the left and the park road leads past picnic areas, toilets and children's playgrounds. The start of the track is signposted from the carpark at the roadend, before the Vaughan Homestead.

TRACK NOTES

- After the 5-minute detour to the gun emplacement, the track passes through coastal forest on a metalled surface. It then undulates over farmland along a grass strip (1 hour). Follow the white banded marker posts. Steps have been constructed on the hilly parts, but the surface can become muddy and slippery after rain.

- At Piripiri Point, the track bears left and after 15 minutes arrives at the Okura River mouth. As an alternative route, 3 hours either side of low tide you can walk around the base of the cliffs to or from Pohutukawa Bay (45 minutes). The rock shelf can be slippery where there is an algal film. Try and pick a route over the barnacle zone (above the oysters), as they provide grip and are a safe distance away from the cliffs where there is danger from falling rocks.

- From Pohutukawa Bay it is a 30-minute walk back to the carpark.

- There is a 15-minute return Nature Walk from near Vaughan Homestead, which follows yellow banded marker posts. It passes through lush puriri and kohekohe-dominated forest and, after the small road bridge, squelches over poorly drained pasture. You are better to turn

The sweeping beach of Long Bay is backed by the extensive grassed areas and facilities of Long Bay Regional Park.

around at the bridge as the forest is the most attractive part of the walk.

POINTS OF INTEREST

- The sandstone and mudstone layers form a striking backdrop to the rock shelf at the cliff base.

- The coastline of the track forms part of the Long Bay–Okura Marine Reserve, established in 1995 to protect all marine life. The interbedded sand and mud cliffs and rocky shoreline are good examples of coastal habitats. The shore becomes progressively less sheltered and this degree of exposure is reflected in the life that abounds there.

- The intertidal zonation of the inhabitants is strikingly evident. Oysters and barnacles rest on the shelf edges, while chitons shelter in rock hollows. Showers of Neptune's necklace adorn the stepped surface. Cats-eyes, periwinkles and whelks are plentiful on the rocks.

- Granny's Bay and Pohutukawa Bay are ideal spots for a picnic. Languid pohutukawa branches provide welcome shade and lazy waves flop to the shore. Pohutukawa Bay is known for nude sunbathing.

- Vaughan Homestead was constructed from local kauri and puriri by George Vaughan in 1862. The dormer windows and wide verandah add character to the building, which has remained intact and is now lovingly restored.

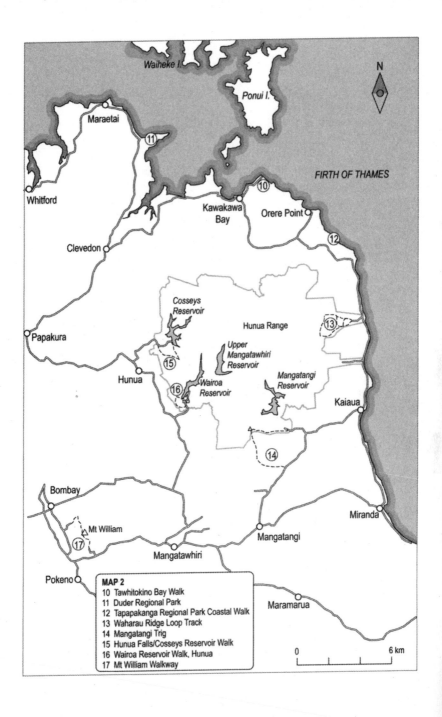

N

Waiheke I.

Ponui I.

FIRTH OF THAMES

Maraetai

⑪

⑩

Whitford

Kawakawa
Bay

Orere Point

⑫

Clevedon

*Cosseys
Reservoir*

Hunua Range

⑬

Papakura

*Upper
Mangatawhiri
Reservoir*

⑮

*Mangatangi
Reservoir*

Hunua

⑯

*Wairoa
Reservoir*

Kaiaua

⑭

Bombay

Mt William

Miranda

⑰

Mangatangi

Pokeno

Mangatawhiri

MAP 2
10 Tawhitokino Bay Walk
11 Duder Regional Park
12 Tapapakanga Regional Park Coastal Walk
13 Waharau Ridge Loop Track
14 Mangatangi Trig
15 Hunua Falls/Cosseys Reservoir Walk
16 Wairoa Reservoir Walk, Hunua
17 Mt William Walkway

Maramarua

0   6 km

SOUTHERN WALKS

Walks in the southern part of the Auckland region are primarily on the Firth of Thames coast and in the Hunua Ranges.

The coastal area has many bays and beaches and the shoreline walks listed here are neither long nor difficult. Nearby to the south is the internationally renowned Miranda Wildlife Reserve, famous as a feeding ground for migrant wading birds, and the Miranda hot pools, which provide an excellent way to relax after a day outdoors.

The Hunua Ranges are part of Auckand City's water catchment area, attracting over 2000 mm of rain per year. The ranges' heavily forested hills and valleys are home to rare wildlife such as kokako and Hochstetter's frog. The area has an extensive track system for the more adventurous, but the walks listed here are the more interesting in the area. A map with all the tracks is available from the Auckland Regional Council.

Two highly recommended walks are:

Tawhitokino Bay Walk (1½ hours return)
A beautiful isolated bay fringed with pohutukawa and swimmable at all tides.

Hunua Falls/Cosseys Reservoir Walk (3 hours loop track)
Beginning at the picturesque Hunua Falls, this walk takes in the reservoir and Cosseys Creek Gorge.

10 Tawhitokino Bay Walk

GRADE 2

TIME 1½ hours return

ACCESS From Kawakawa Bay, follow Kawakawa Bay Coast Road for 4.3 km to the carpark at Waiti Bay. The road hovers above the idyllic indentations of the coastline under a canopy of pohutukawa. At Waiti Bay there is a good beach for swimming, as well as toilets and picnic benches. The start of the track is signposted along the beach to the right.

TRACK NOTES

○ Cross the rocky headland to the south and walk along the fine sands of Tuturau Bay. At the far side of the small creek after the bach, a stepped track climbs the headland behind Papanui Point. For the final 30 minutes you are shrouded in the shade of regenerating coastal forest. The track is stepped but can be slippery, with muddy hollows between steps.

POINTS OF INTEREST

○ The walk is a mix of colourful rocky headlands, secluded sandy coves and cool shaded forest.

○ The views out across the Gulf to the outer islands and over to the Coromandel Peninsula are stunning.

○ The bountiful rockpools of the headlands are filled with marine life and interesting to sift through.

○ Large spreading pohutukawa cool the rear of the sandy beaches, which merge with the coastal forest where tui flock in the flowering kowhai and New Zealand pigeon swoop above the rewarewa.

○ Tawhitokino Bay's beach is long and gently sloping, and perfect for swimming at all tides. There is a basic campground further down the beach, with running water and a long-drop toilet.

11 Duder Regional Park

GRADE 2

TIME 3 hours return

ACCESS From Clevedon, follow North Road 10 km. Duder Regional Park is signposted on the right, 1 km before Umupuia Beach. The start

The headland of Duder Regional Park juts into the Hauraki Gulf.

of the track is signposted from the carpark, which also has toilets nearby.

TRACK NOTES

○ The walk is a combination of two tracks. The Farm Loop is indicated by red banded marker poles and the Whakakaiwhara Pa Walk is shown by blue banded marker poles. The walks cross open pasture and follow established farm tracks excavated into the hillside. These tend to collect water after periods of rain.

○ Shortly after leaving the carpark, head left and climb to the trig station. The track then hugs the ridge and after 45 minutes meets the junction with the Whakakaiwhara Pa Walk. This takes 1 hour return and funnels to a knife-blade ridge at the pa site on the extremity of the headland.

○ The return walk follows the Farm Loop over a metalled farm road for the final 15 minutes. There is a 15-minute-return detour through the coastal forest to some sandy bays at the foot of the cliffs. Head left on reaching sea level and double back along the coast.

POINTS OF INTEREST

○ The peninsula forming the regional park was the first landing place in the Waitemata Harbour of the *Tainui* canoe. The headland pa commanded extensive views for Ngai Tai residents of the Hauraki Gulf coastline and offshore islands. The pa was named Whaka-kai-whara, which means 'eat the bracts of the kiekie vine'.

○ Near the top of the site is a defensive ditch, used to protect the dwellings and kumara storage pits. These well-preserved hollows litter the highest points of the headland.

○ In 1866, Thomas Duder purchased 243 hectares of land from Ngai Tai and farmed it. Pockets of native forest are fenced from grazing stock and include young kauri. A ring of pohutukawa surrounds the peninsula.

○ The coastal views encompass many Hauraki Gulf islands, including Pakihi, Ponui and Waiheke. The multitude of islands and the distant Coromandel Range enclose the sea views and give the impression of looking at a large lake. Ridges of shells shelter extensive salt marshes to the south of the headland.

12 Tapapakanga Regional Park Coastal Walk

GRADE 2

TIME 2½ hours (return via Farm Route)

ACCESS Tapapakanga Regional Park is 18 km from Kaiaua and 28 km from Clevedon along East Coast Road. The park entrance is signposted. Pass through the intricately carved pou (poles) and follow the unsealed road to the carpark. The start of the walk is signposted.

TRACK NOTES

○ The Coastal Walk is marked by red banded posts, and the Farm Route by orange banded posts. There is also a separate mountain bike trail marked by yellow banded posts.

○ From the carpark by the homestead, the coastal walk follows the rocky beach to Tapapakanga Stream. If the tide is high and there has been recent heavy rain, you may have to deviate inland along the farm track and use the ford. This alternative route rejoins the coastal track by the cemetery.

○ The track then weaves through pockets of coastal forest and along fencelines bordering the paddocks.

○ After approximately 1 hour, the track heads inland through sheep

From Tapapakanga Regional Park you can see the Coromandel Range across the Hauraki Gulf.

paddocks to a trig station. The return Farm Route is clearly marked and follows the ridgeline to the gully of the Tapapakanga Stream.

POINTS OF INTEREST

○ The land was settled by Maori, who took advantage of the abundant food sources and prominent headland pa sites. Prehistoric stone-field gardens flank the entrance road after entering the park.

○ In 1899, James and Rebecca Ashby bought land and forged a strong friendship with the local Maori chief, Tukumana Taiwiwi te Taniwha. Timber felled in the clearing of the land was sold to Auckland mills and the profit shared jointly.

○ The Ashbys built the fine kauri homestead still in existence today and raised 14 children. The family cemetery is beside the track after crossing Tapapakanga Stream.

○ The coastal cliffs support some stately pohutukawa trees. Look also for the rare stand of taraire near the start of the climb to the trig.

○ Occasional glimpses of the Coromandel Range shimmer over the hazy waters of the Hauraki Gulf.

13 Waharau Ridge Loop Track

GRADE 2

TIME 3–4 hours

ACCESS This track begins in the upper carpark just past the information kiosk in the Waharau Regional Park on the East Coast Road north of Kaiaua on the Firth of Thames.

TRACK NOTES

○ A well-formed track links with the Waharau Ridge Track to form a loop back to the carpark. Two other interconnecting tracks mean that this trip can be considerably shortened to suit your party. The climb to the ridge is even and not too demanding.

POINTS OF INTEREST

○ About halfway on this walk on the Waharau Ridge Track is a pleasant clearing with extensive views over the Firth of Thames and Coromandel. This is the ideal spot for a lunch break.

14 Mangatangi Trig

GRADE 3

TIME 4–5 hours

ACCESS Mangatangi Trig can be accessed via either the Vining Track or the Mangatangi Trig Track. The Vining Track starting point is off the Kaiaua road heading east from Mangatangi, just after Fern Road. The Mangatangi Trig Track is off Workman Road. You will need to return the way you came unless you have a car at either end.

TRACK NOTES

○ The Vining Track begins on farmland and then enters bush for a steady uphill climb to the trig where it links up with the Mangatangi Trig Track.

○ The Mangatangi Trig Track from Workman Road is the shorter route and, like the Vining Track, is a steady uphill climb. The Vining Track is closed for lambing in August and September.

POINTS OF INTEREST

○ Mangatangi is 487 m high. There are extensive views to the south over the Waikato, east to the Firth of Thames and north over the Hunua Ranges.

15 Hunua Falls/Cosseys Reservoir Walk

GRADE 2

TIME 3 hours return

ACCESS This loop track begins at the Hunua Falls carpark. From Hunua Village head north and just past the park information building turn right into White Road. After 1.1 km turn right into Falls Road and the carpark is another 2.2 km.

TRACK NOTES

○ From the carpark cross the bridge and follow the Cosseys Gorge Track. After about 400 m take the Massey Track that leads off to the right, climbing uphill. At the intersection of the Wairoa–Cosseys Track turn left down to Cosseys Reservoir. From the reservoir the Cosseys Gorge Track takes you back to the carpark.

Hunua Falls/Cosseys Reservoir Walk. Peter Janssen

POINTS OF INTEREST

○ The Hunua Falls are worth a visit in their own right and after heavy rain can be quite spectacular. The falls (28 m) flow over a hard basalt plug which is part of the northern rim of an ancient volcano.

○ Just over the bridge a track leads to the right and leads to an upper lookout (15 minutes return) and a lower lookout at the base of the falls on the eastern side (10 minutes return). Tawa is the dominant tree in this area and a number of fine examples are found along the track.

○ There is a grove of kauri near the intersection of the Wairoa–Cosseys/Massey tracks that is worth visiting.

○ Just before reaching the dam a lookout point gives extensive views north over the reservoir.

○ The return trip along the Cosseys Gorge Track follows the stream through attractive bush.

○ There are good toilet and picnic facilities by the waterfall.

Hunua Falls/Cosseys Reservoir Walk. Peter Janssen

16 Wairoa Reservoir Walk, Hunua

GRADE 2

TIME 1 hour 45 minutes

ACCESS From Hunua village head south along Hunua Road for 6 km and turn left into Moumoukai Road. After 1.5 km the road divides; take the left-hand road to the Wairoa Dam; the other road leads to the Manga-tawhiri Dam. The carpark is immediately to your left opposite the information board.

TRACK NOTES

○ From the carpark walk up the road to the suspension bridge and follow the Suspension Bridge Track as it climbs steadily along the ridge to the Wairoa–Cosseys Track. Turn right and walk back down to the dam road and carpark.

POINTS OF INTEREST

○ About 30 minutes along the Suspension Bridge Track you come to a lookout giving 360-degree views over lush farmland to the south and west, and over the ranges and the Wairoa dam to the north and west. A further lookout just before the dam gives an excellent view of the dam and the lake.

○ Completed in 1975, the dam is of earth fill construction using local greywacke. An information board can be found on the western side of the dam.

○ The suspension bridge is about 25 metres above the bush-covered stream.

○ There are good picnic facilities and toilets.

17 Mount William Walkway

GRADE 2

TIME 2 hours return

ACCESS Take the Bombay exit off the Southern Motorway, turn right into Razorback Road, then left into Puketutu Road. The beginning of the track is well marked on Puketutu Road. There is another access point at McMillan Road, which leads off Irish Road, to the left off State Highway 2 not far from the intersection with State Highway 1, but the Puketutu entrance is the much easier option.

TRACK NOTES

○ An easy walk over farmland to Mount William. For the energetic there is a loop track through the bush area on the southern slopes below Mount William, which will take a further hour.

POINTS OF INTEREST

○ Walking through open country makes a pleasant change from the usual bush tracks of the Auckland area. The views from Mount William (369 m) are extensive to the south over the Waikato and north to Auckland. A side-track to the left leads up to the rocky peak of Puketutu (376 m).

○ The bush in the scenic reserve is notable for containing a mixture of kauri and beech.

18 Awhitu Regional Park Farm Walk

GRADE 2

TIME 1½ hours return

ACCESS From Waiuku, follow Awhitu Road 33 km over steep farmland to Brooks Road. Awhitu Regional Park is signposted. Near the carpark are toilets, picnic tables, barbecues and a campground. The start of the track is signposted just below the carpark.

TRACK NOTES

○ The Farm Walk is lined with yellow banded marker posts. Red banded posts indicate the shorter Brooks Homestead Walk.

○ A wide, well-formed track descends to Kauritutahi Beach and follows a mown grass strip behind the white sand. Opposite the jetty the track climbs to the Brooks Homestead.

○ Descend to Brooks Beach, which shelters a thriving wetland, before traversing farmland to the lookout at the top of the hill.

○ The loop rejoins the track behind Brooks Beach. An alternative route to the carpark follows the road on the left before Brooks Homestead.

POINTS OF INTEREST

○ Brooks Homestead is perched on solid brick piles and surrounded by gardens filled with mature northern hemisphere trees and a massive macrocarpa. Pitsawn kauri from Orua Bay was used to clad the sturdy structure and the building still sits elegantly in its peaceful setting.

John and Sarah Brooks settled the land and farmed it with their five children. The family lived there until 1971.

○ The Awhitu Peninsula was mainly inhabited by Ngati Te Ata iwi. They fished the extensive tidal flats in Manukau Harbour on the sheltered eastern side of the peninsula. At high tide these flats form shallow bays, good for swimming.

○ Kauritutahi Beach and Brooks Beach harbour thriving wetlands. Emergent kahikatea forests rise to rich green pastures on the hillsides. From Brooks Beach there is an old jetty running out towards Kauritutahi Island.

○ The excited shrill calls of South Island pied oystercatchers pierce the air. Other waders include pied stilts and, in summer, godwits. Banded rail and fernbirds inhabit the reeds and rushes of the wetlands. There is a complement of tui and New Zealand pigeon in the enclave of preserved coastal forest.

○ The Awhitu Peninsula was formed 2 million years ago as a climatic epoch of southwesterly winds blew inland to form massive dunes. These have since consolidated to form the peninsula, which acts as a barrier to create the Manukau Harbour.

○ While visiting the Awhitu area you should take a drive to the light-house at the northern tip at Manukau Heads, and across to Orua Bay, with its golden sands and beautiful swimming beach. The wild west coast is worth a visit too — great raw cliffs rising out of black sand, constantly eroded by wind and water. The coast is accessed down West Coast Road.

WESTERN WALKS

Few cities in the world are fortunate to have a wildness area less than one hour's drive from downtown. Waterfalls, wild surf beaches, forest streams, magnificent rainforest and stunning views are features of the Waitakere Ranges, which contain some of the best walks in Auckland.

Human occupation goes back almost 1000 years, with this area being the ancestral home of the iwi Te Kawerau a Maki. Farming and the logging industry in the early nineteenth century dramatically changed the landscape and much of the area contains regenerating forest.

The area is literally laced with walkways and tracks and this book offers what we consider the pick of the bunch. Highly recommended is a visit to the Arataki Environment and Heritage Centre on Scenic Drive between Titirangi and Waiatarua. Opposite the centre is an easy short walk, the Arataki Nature Trail, which is recommended as an ideal introduction to the native flora and fauna of the area. For those who wish to explore further the centre also has for sale a detailed map of all the tracks in the area.

Highly recommended walks are:

Lake Wainamu Walkway (2–3 hours return)
Follow in the footsteps of *Xena, Warrior Princess*, across barren sand dunes to a lake that is ideal for a swim and a picnic.

Cascade Kauri, Auckland City Walk, Waitakere Ranges Regional Park (1 hour return) An easy walk on a well-formed track, with beautiful native bush lining the Waitakere Stream. The highlight is two magnificent kauri, which somehow escaped the attention of early loggers.

Mercer Bay Loop Walk (1½ hours)
Magnificent coastal scenery from Te Ahua Point, with huge cliffs dropping off into a wild sea. The track is well formed and well marked.

Whatipu–Gibbons Track (6 hours return)
For the more adventurous, this trip combines great coastal scenery with a taste of wild New Zealand, especially when there is a strong southwesterly blowing.

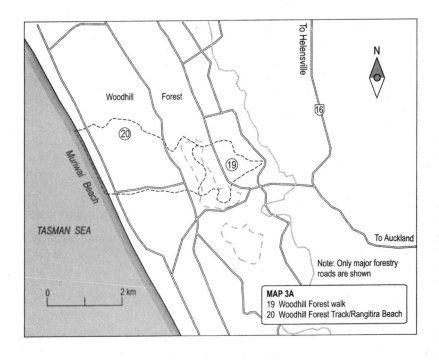

Woodhill Forest

To Helensville

N

16

Munwai Beach

20

19

TASMAN SEA

To Auckland

Note: Only major forestry
roads are shown

0   2 km

MAP 3A
19 Woodhill Forest walk
20 Woodhill Forest Track/Rangitira Beach

19 Woodhill Forest Walk

GRADE 2

TIME $2\frac{1}{2}$ hours

ACCESS Take State Highway 16 towards Helensville. The entrance to Woodhill Forest is clearly marked 6 km past the Muriwai turnoff at Waimauku. Turn left into Restall Road, and after 1.5 km turn right into Boundary Road. Park at the picnic area on the right 1 km down Boundary Road. The track starts opposite the carpark.

TRACK NOTES

- This track is exceptionally well marked and forms a loop through pine forest and native bush and then returns to the carpark.

- Keep an eye out for mountain bikes and motorcycles when using forestry roads in the area.

- Access to this area is with the kind permission of Carter Holt Harvey Ltd.

POINTS OF INTEREST

- This track is suitable all year round as the area is sand dunes.

- The native bush is unusual in that it contains species that have adapted to the dry and sandy soils of the old sand dune country. The dominant species is kanuka, with occasional rewarewa, but ground species include kawakawa, small-leaved coprosmas, kidney fern and mosses.

20 Woodhill Forest Track/Rangitira Beach

GRADE 3

TIME 5 hours return

ACCESS Take State Highway 16 towards Helensville. The entrance to Woodhill Forest is clearly marked 6 km past the Muriwai turnoff at Waimauku. Turn left into Restall Road, and after 1.5 km turn right into Boundary Road. Park at the picnic area on the right 1 km down Boundary Road. The track starts opposite the carpark.

TRACK NOTES

- The initial part of this track is the same as the Woodhill Forest Walk. However, where the track divides just after you come out of the native bush, take the track to the left and follow the markers until you reach the beach. If the tide is high or the conditions rough making the beach route unsafe, an alternative route along a forestry road is clearly marked.

○ Once on the beach, head north until you see the markers high on the sand hills. There are couple of points that look like the track but will lead you nowhere so double check you have the right place.

○ Once you have left the beach make sure you follow the markers as this section of the track is a maze of roads, tracks and trails and it is easy to lose your bearings. The track back to the carpark is very clearly marked and as long as you follow these you won't get lost.

POINTS OF INTEREST

○ Where the beach forms part of the track is a quiet part of Muriwai Beach and is ideal for a picnic away from the crowds. The sea in this area is notoriously dangerous so be extremely careful when swimming.

○ You are likely to meet riders on horseback at some point on this track. Also keep an eye out for cars and motorbikes on the main forestry roads.

21 Mokoroa Falls and Goldies Bush

GRADE 2 (direct route)

3 (return route via stream)

TIME 1 hour return to the falls by the most direct route. Three hours return for the round trip via the stream. Do not attempt the stream track if it is in flood.

ACCESS The beginning of the track is clearly marked at the end of Horseman Road.

TRACK NOTES

○ The most direct route to the falls is downhill from the carpark and takes about 1 hour return. Although clearly marked, it is not well formed and is very slippery when wet and virtually unusable in winter. A lookout point gives a good view of the falls and pool. A track to the left of the lookout leads down to the pool at the bottom of the falls.

○ The walk via the stream takes about 3 hours return and involves multiple stream crossings and rockhopping. It could be considered a Grade 3 track (you will get your feet wet). As it is easier to do this trip upstream than downstream, take the track that leads off the main track to the left, about 300 m down from the carpark. Follow this track downhill until you reach the stream (about 30 minutes), and then follow the stream up to the falls.

○ Although the stream track is marked, it is hard to find the markers in some places, especially where the track follows the actual streambed. The track criss-crosses the stream numerous times, and is never far from it. It pays to check from time to time that you are still on the track.

○ Another entrance to this area is off Oaia Road via Muriwai. This track is clearly marked and begins with a long downhill walk taking around 30 minutes before you reach the stream. Of course, if you come back this way you finish the trip on the long uphill.

POINTS OF INTEREST

○ There are actually two waterfalls that flow into a single pool with a pleasant picnic spot at the bottom of the waterfall. As well as the waterfall pool there are numerous pools along the stream that are safe for swimming.

○ The stream track passes through a mysterious grove of nikau, and another almost totally of mahoe (whiteywood) with a carpet of papery leaves underfoot.

○ Look out for cockabullies and eels in the stream. If you're lucky, you might even spot a koura (freshwater crayfish).

22 Takapu Refuge Walk

GRADE 2

TIME 30 minutes return

ACCESS From the carpark at the end of Motutara Road in Muriwai, follow the boardwalk up Otakamiro Point. There are toilets, barbecues and picnic tables at the carpark.

Alternatively, follow signposts along Waitea Road to the gannet colony and the carpark above Maori Bay.

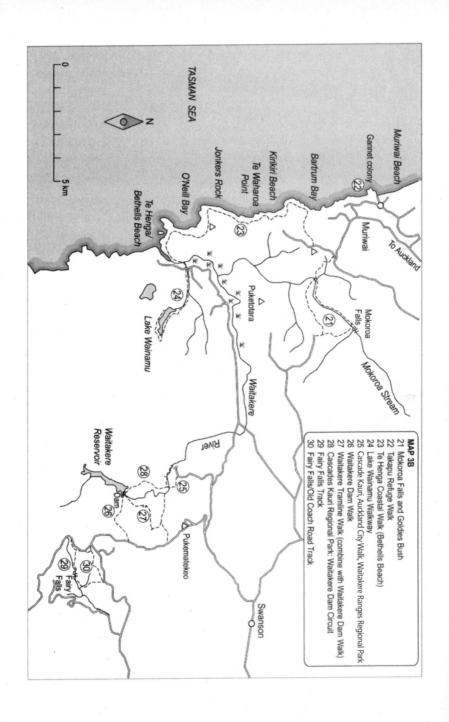

TASMAN SEA

Muriwai Beach
Gannet colony
(22)
Bartrum Bay
Te Waharoa Point
Kirikiri Beach
Jonkers Rock
O'Neill Bay
Te Henga/Bethells Beach
(23)
(24)
Lake Wainamu
Puketotara
Muriwai
To Auckland
Mokoroa Falls
(21)
Mokoroa Stream
Waitakere River
Waitakere Reservoir
(28)
Dam
(26)
(25)
(27)
Pukematekeo
Swanson
Fairy Falls
(29)
(30)

0
5 km
N

MAP 3B
21 Mokoroa Falls and Goldies Bush
22 Takapu Refuge Walk
23 Te Henga Coastal Walk (Bethells Beach)
24 Lake Wainamu Walkway
25 Cascade Kauri, Auckland City Walk, Waitakere Ranges Regional Park
26 Waitakere Dam Walk
27 Waitakere Tramline Walk (combine with Waitakere Dam Walk)
28 Cascades Kauri Regional Park: Waitakere Dam Circuit
29 Fairy Falls Track
30 Fairy Falls/Old Coach Road Track

TRACK NOTES

○ From the southern end of Muriwai Beach, the boardwalk snakes up to two lookout platforms, each perched on the tip of a headland. The second, above Motutara Island, can also be reached via an even, metalled track 5 minutes from the carpark at Maori Bay.

○ A return route descends through native forest past enormous pohutukawa. The Maori Bay Track, which is signposted from the road to the Maori Bay carpark, leads down to the main Motutara Road carpark on a well-formed surface.

POINTS OF INTEREST

○ The Takapu Refuge was established in 1979 to protect the expanding breeding population of takapu (Australasian gannets, *Morus serrator*), which were nesting on Oaia Island, 1.6 km offshore.

○ With increased numbers, the gannets have displaced the white-fronted terns from Motutara ('island of terns') Island and formed their distinctive mounded nests atop the spectacular rock stack.

○ The gannets are majestic fliers and can often be seen diving with aerobatic precision to catch their prey. They breed in New Zealand and, after fledging, spend two to three years around Australia before

If you take a short walk from the southern end of Muriwai Beach, you will be rewarded with the sight of the beautiful Australasian gannets in residence at the Takapu Refuge.

Te Henga Coastal Walk (Bethells Beach).

returning. Between July and January you can observe the gannets as they return to their original breeding grounds, establish partnerships, breed, nest and rear their chicks. The viewing platforms allow you to observe courtship displays, aggressive territorial squabbles (with bills locked amid much wing flapping) and rearing of nestlings.

○ The updraught from the cliffs is also harnessed by the birds to aid take-off. You can watch them swoop and glide before deftly alighting on the hummocky terrain of their nesting grounds.

○ Above Maori Bay, interesting rock formations in the cliffs give clues to their geological past. The radiating spikes of angular rock are known as pillow lava and formed during the undersea eruption of molten rock.

○ On contact with cold water, the outer skin of a lava bubble cools, while the enclosed molten rock continues to flow under pressure. It penetrates a weakness in the shell of rock and explodes like a water-filled balloon, forming a pillow shape. The examples of the differing-sized pillows preserved in the cliffs above Maori Bay are world-renowned.

23 Te Henga Coastal Walk (Bethells Beach)

GRADE 2

TIME 3 hours one way to Constable Road

ACCESS The beginning of the walk at Bethells is clearly marked at the bridge carpark about 1 km from the beach and opposite the entrance to Lake Wainamu.

TRACK NOTES

○ After crossing the Waitakere River this undulating coastal walkway goes all the way to Muriwai Beach. The track is well marked but steep in sections and you have to return the same way unless you have transport organised at the other end. The walk is mainly on clifftops and the coast is very exposed so make sure you have warm clothing.

POINTS OF INTEREST

○ The swamp at the beginning of the walk is one of the richest wetland areas in the Auckland region and home to a wide range of wildlife including several rare bird species.

○ The coastal scenery is spectacular, typical of the wild open west coast. This is an ideal walk to get away from it all. If you don't have transport at the other end it is still worth walking part of the way and returning to Bethells.

24 Lake Wainamu Walkway

GRADE 2

TIME 2–3 hours return

ACCESS The entrance to the track is clearly marked to the left of the bridge about 1 km from the beach carpark. Te Henga Coastal Walk (see previous entry) starts opposite.

TRACK NOTES

○ Initially following the Waiti Stream the track then follows the northern (left) shoreline of the lake and eventually crosses the Wainamu Stream. Part of the southern shoreline of the lake is in private ownership, so the official track returns the same way, but an unofficial track continues right around the lake.

POINTS OF INTEREST

○ Spectacular black sand dunes have blocked the stream to form the lake and these dunes are worth a visit in themselves. The young at heart will enjoy sliding down the steep slopes. Many of the location shoots for *Xena, Warrior Princess* and *Hercules* were filmed in this area and will be recognisable to fans of the series.

Lake Wainamu Walkway. Peter Janssen

○ The Wainamu Stream at the head of the lake is worth exploring, with many attractive deep rockpools and small waterfalls. There is an excellent swimming hole below the falls at the lake end of the stream.

○ The lake is ideal for swimming at the dune end, but be aware that it drops off steeply and is very deep.

25 Cascade Kauri, Auckland City Walk, Waitakere Ranges Regional Park

GRADE 1

TIME 1 hour return

ACCESS Take Te Henga Road between Scenic Drive and Bethells Beach and, after a few kilometres, turn left into Falls Road. Drive down Falls Road, through the golf course to the carpark. A gateway and information board marks the entrance to the walk, which drops downhill to the swingbridge over Waitakere Stream.

TRACK NOTES

○ One of the best formed and maintained tracks in the area and very clearly marked. Suitable for all ages and levels of fitness. It is a loop track and returns to the carpark.

POINTS OF INTEREST

○ This walk is very picturesque, especially the first section. After crossing the swingbridge the track follows the Waitakere Stream, which is lined with superb native bush, including nikau palms and large treeferns.

○ A feature of the walk is the number of kauri trees, including two that are possibly the largest in the Auckland region. These and other features of the bush are well signposted with interpretive panels.

○ A short side-walk to the Cascades Waterfall is disappointing as the waterfall is almost entirely hidden in a small gorge.

○ This is one of the best spots to take international visitors who wish to experience New Zealand bush but who may be short on time. There are pleasant grassed areas by the carpark suitable for picnics, with plenty of space for children to run around.

26 Waitakere Dam Walk

GRADE 1

TIME 1¼ hours return

ACCESS The walk begins on Scenic Drive, 7 km north of the Piha Road/Scenic Drive intersection, or 1.5 km past Mountain Road, at the large carpark on the left.

TRACK NOTES

○ A wide sealed road leads down to the Waitakere Dam. Return to the carpark the same way (or see Waitakere Tramline Walk, next entry). There are toilets at the bottom of the road, just above the dam.

POINTS OF INTEREST

○ An easy walk for all ages.

○ The Waitakere Dam, at the head of a valley with extensive views to the north, is one of the oldest water reservoirs in the Auckland area.

○ The bush that borders the road to the dam is rich and varied, with a fine burst of scarlet in late summer when the rata is in flower. A short track to the left halfway down leads to a giant kauri.

○ Tui gather in the trees at the base of the dam, and kereru sweep across the valley.

27 Waitakere Tramline Walk (combine with the Waitakere Dam Walk)

GRADE 2

TIME 2 hours return

ACCESS This track is a continuation of the Waitakere Dam Walk.

TRACK NOTES

○ After reaching the dam via the Waitakere Dam Walk, this track begins at the base of the dam and follows the tram- and pipeline to the West Tunnel Track, which in turn joins the Anderson Track leading back to Scenic Drive. It is a 15-minute walk back up the road to the carpark.

POINTS OF INTEREST

○ The tramline track follows a ledge with great views across the Waitakere Valley to the north and west and down to the tops of nikau and treeferns far below. The short tramline tunnel is an added attraction (no torch necessary).

○ At Picnic Flats station there is a shelter, with a small grass clearing and picnic table.

28 Cascades Kauri Regional Park: Waitakere Dam Circuit

GRADE 2

TIME 3 hours return

ACCESS Take Te Henga Road between Scenic Drive and Bethells Beach and, after a few kilometres, turn left into Falls Road. Drive down Falls Road, through the golf course to the carpark. A gateway and information board marks the entrance to the walk, which drops downhill to the swingbridge over Waitakere Stream.

TRACK NOTES

○ This loop walk combines a number of shorter walks in the area to take in the key features. Take the Auckland City Walk to the Fenceline Track which leads off to the right and climb steeply up a ridge through regenerating kauri. Where the Fenceline Track meets the Waitakere Dam Walk turn left and then left again on to the Waitakere Tramline Track. Return to the carpark via the West Tunnel Mouth Track, the Anderson Track and the Auckland City Walk. It can also be done from the other end, beginning at Scenic Drive and Waitakere Dam (see Waitakere Dam Walk, page 56).

POINTS OF INTEREST

○ This longer walk includes all the features of the Auckland City Walk, the Waitakere Dam and Waitakere Tramline Walks.

29 Fairy Falls Track

GRADE 2

TIME 1 hour return

ACCESS Heading north along Scenic Drive the track begins opposite the carpark, which is on the left-hand side of the road 4.7 km from the Scenic Drive/Piha Road intersection and just before Mountain Road. There is a toilet at the start of the track.

TRACK NOTES

○ Well-formed track, initially flat but then descending steeply, including stairs and a boardwalk going down beside the falls.

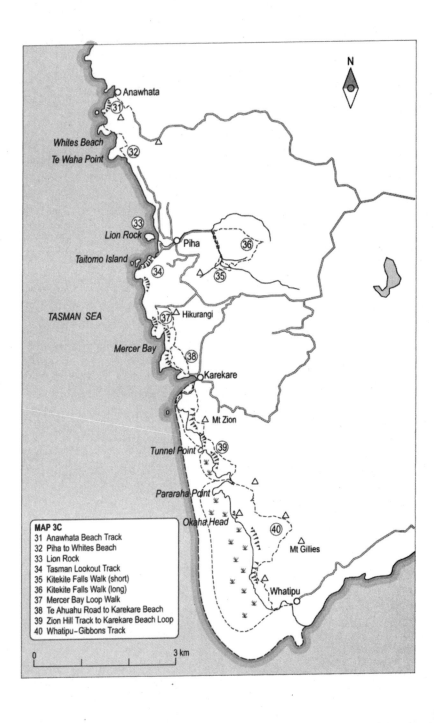

N

Anawhata
○ ③①
△

Whites Beach
△
Te Waha Point ③②

③③
Lion Rock
○ Piha
Taitomo Island ③⑥
③④ △ ③⑤

TASMAN SEA
③⑦ ⊢ Hikurangi

Mercer Bay
③⑧
○ Karekare

△ Mt Zion
Tunnel Point ③⑨

Pararaha Point

Okaha Head ④⓪

△ Mt Gillies

MAP 3C
31 Anawhata Beach Track
32 Piha to Whites Beach
33 Lion Rock
34 Tasman Lookout Track
35 Kitekite Falls Walk (short)
36 Kitekite Falls Walk (long)
37 Mercer Bay Loop Walk
38 Te Ahuahu Road to Karekare Beach
39 Zion Hill Track to Karekare Beach Loop
40 Whatipu–Gibbons Track

○ Whatipu

0   3 km

POINTS OF INTEREST

○ One of the prettiest waterfalls in the Auckland area with water cascading down a wide rock face. Well worth the visit.

30 Fairy Falls/Old Coach Road Track

GRADE 2

TIME 2 hours

ACCESS As for the Fairy Falls Track (previous entry).

TRACK NOTES

○ This loop track crosses the stream at the base of the falls and continues on to Mountain Road. A short distance up the road, the track re-enters the bush as Old Coach Road Track. Follow this track uphill to where it exits on Scenic Drive, about half a kilometre below the carpark. There is an extension that runs beside Scenic Drive through the bush to join up with the start of the Fairy Falls Track.

POINTS OF INTEREST

○ The Old Coach Road Track is noted for its large rimu and kauri.

31 Anawhata Beach Track

GRADE 3

TIME 45 minutes return

ACCESS The start of the track is signposted from the end of Anawhata Road.

TRACK NOTES

○ The track is mostly metalled as it drops steeply to the beach through low, windswept vegetation.

POINTS OF INTEREST

○ Anawhata Beach is a mystical, raw stretch of coarse sand, with unusual rock formations.

○ Swimming is possible in the river, just inland from the beach.

32 Piha to Whites Beach

GRADE 3

TIME 1½ hours return

ACCESS The start of the track is signposted on the right at the northern end of Piha Beach. You can park in the northernmost parking area and walk along the beach past the caves to the start of the walk.

TRACK NOTES

○ The track is signposted, even and well formed. It climbs via the Laird Thomson Track for 15 minutes to the junction with a lookout (5 minutes return) on the headland. Then head right for 10 minutes to where the Rose Track is signposted on the left. It's a further 15 minutes down to Whites Beach.

○ There is a track leading from the junction with the lookout track, straight down to the beach. However, it is very steep and quite unstable, and is not recommended.

POINTS OF INTEREST

○ Whites Beach was named after John White, a keen ethnographer who was passionate about Maori culture, and negotiated the initial sale of coastal land from the Maori.

The striking form of Nun Rock at Piha Beach.

Whites Beach is a great reward for climbing over the northern headland at Piha.

○ It is a secluded beach with tan and black sand. Steep cliffs smothered in flax, manuka, kawakawa and pohutukawa rise abruptly from the beach. A steady haze of salt spray billows up the hillside, fuelled by the ever-present wind. There is a deep sea-cave on the northern side.

○ The beach is a popular venue for environmental sculptures to be temporarily erected and reclaimed by the elements.

○ The views from the headland lookout and the track itself are expansive and stunning.

33 Lion Rock

GRADE 2

TIME 15 minutes return

ACCESS Lion Rock is a prominent landmark at the mouth of the Piha Stream. There is ample parking on the beachfront on Seaview Road.

TRACK NOTES
○ A popular walk for many years, much of the top section is now closed.

POINTS OF INTEREST

○ Lion Rock stands like a sentry and dominates the black sands of Piha Beach. It rises in an unabated cliff and is capped with a sprinkling of vegetation.

○ To Te Kawerau a Maki, Lion Rock was an important defensive pa. The tihi (pinnacle) at the summit was the last line of defence in case of invasion. It was called Te Piha after the wave patterns on its seaward side, which resemble those of the bow-wave of a waka.

○ Lion Rock is an offshore stack, formed from the relentless action of wave and wind. Its resistant cap of rock has withstood erosion, while weaker rocks around have been steadily dismantled.

34 Tasman Lookout Track

GRADE 2

TIME 30 minutes return

ACCESS The start of the track is signposted from the southern end of Piha Beach. There is parking nearby.

TRACK NOTES

○ The wide, well-formed, even track is aided with steps as it climbs via a lookout to a bench above The Gap.

POINTS OF INTEREST

○ The Gap is the name given to a break in the rocks between Taitomo Island and the rock shelf on the mainland.

○ When there is a sizeable swell, cataclysmic explosions of froth are forced through the narrow gap and provide an awe-inspiring spectacle. Other nearby crevices show the embryonic stages of the same feature. In time the cracks in the rock will be enlarged to form caverns, the roofs of which will collapse to form offshore stacks.

○ From the lookout there are magnificent views all the way up Piha Beach.

35 Kitekite Falls Walk (short)

GRADE 1

TIME 1 hour return

ACCESS Take the road to Piha and at the bottom of the hill just before the bridge turn right into Glen Esk Road. The carpark is at the end of Glen Esk Road and the track begins to the right.

TRACK NOTES

○ A flat well-formed loop track follows the Glen Esk Stream to the base of the falls, crosses the stream and returns down the other side. The top of the falls is reached by a steep track (Connect Track), which begins about 100 m from the base of the waterfall on the north side of the stream. It will take about 15 minutes to get to the top.

POINTS OF INTEREST

○ Pretty waterfall and stream walk with attractive native bush as a bonus. Suitable for all the family.

○ The pool below the falls is good for swimming, though very cold.

36 Kitekite Falls Walk (long)

GRADE 2

TIME 3 hours return

ACCESS Take the road to Piha and at the bottom of the hill just before the bridge turn right into Glen Esk Road. The carpark is at the end of Glen Esk Road and the track begins to the right.

TRACK NOTES

○ This walk is a continuation of the short walk and returns in a loop to the carpark. Take the Connect Track, which begins about 100 m from the base of the waterfall on the north side of the stream and climbs steeply to the top of the falls. Turn left when you reach the Winstone Track and left again onto the Home Track, which takes you back to the carpark.

POINTS OF INTEREST

○ Just above the waterfall are four large grooves cut into the rock. These grooves once formed the base of a kauri dam designed to block the flow of water in order to float kauri logs downstream.

○ Fine stands of young kauri are found on the Home Track.

Stoney Batter Walkway, Waiheke Island.

37 Mercer Bay Loop Walk

GRADE 2

TIME 1½ hours return

ACCESS The beginning of the track is on the northwest side of the carpark at the end of Te Ahuahu Road/Log Race Road, which turns left off Piha Road just before the road descends to Piha.

TRACK NOTES

○ A well-marked, well-formed track follows the clifftop down to Te Ahua Point. You can return the same way or take the right-hand track at the junction and then turn left and go back uphill to the carpark.

POINTS OF INTEREST

○ One of the best short coastal walks in the Auckland area.

○ The track is generally open, allowing the walker to take full advantage of the superb views.

○ Huge cliffs tower above a wild sea with views on a good day as far south as Mount Karioi.

38 Te Ahuahu Road to Karekare Beach

GRADE 3

TIME 1½ hours one way; 3 hours return

ACCESS From Piha Road at the top of the hill before descending to the settlement, turn into Te Ahuahu Road (which turns into Log Race Road) and follow it 1.3 km to the roadend carpark. Take the signposted Mercer Bay Loop Walk at the northern side of the carpark.

At Karekare, there is a parking area on the right by Watchmans Road before the main carpark at Karekare Beach.

TRACK NOTES

○ This walk is an amalgamation of the Mercer Bay Loop Walk, Te Ahuahu Track and Colman's Track. The tracks are unmarked, but well signposted and well formed.

○ From the northern (Piha) side of the parking area at the end of Log Race Road by the tower, follow Mercer Bay Loop Walk 15 minutes to the junction with the detour to the lookout at Te Ahua Point (10 minutes return).

○ Continue on, past the junction with Mercer Bay Loop Walk where it returns to Te Ahuahu Road and, at the Te Ahuahu Track, bear right. This section of the track can be muddy.

○ After 2 minutes the track forks. Take a right fork, signposted along Colman's Track. It is 45 minutes along the ridge to Karekare Beach.

POINTS OF INTEREST

○ From Te Ahua Point and the other lookouts on the ridge above the sea, the sheer cliffs rise so steeply no vegetation can take hold.

○ Frothing seas pummel the base of the cliffs and only the tan and black sands of Mercer Bay and Karekare break the dramatic cliffs.

○ The vegetation is a low regenerating remnant of flax, kawakawa and pohutukawa with occasional groves of puriri and nikau.

TRACK NOTES

○ To make this a loop trip, retrace your steps and come back over the small hill from the beach. Take the track that leads to the right. Where the Green's Track goes off to the left, continue straight ahead on Te Ahuahu Track, which climbs steadily up the eastern side of the ridge to rejoin the Mercer Bay Loop Walk back to the carpark.

39 Zion Hill Track to Karekare Beach Loop

GRADE 3

TIME 4 hours return

ACCESS The start of the track is signposted from the carpark over the Company Stream bridge behind Karekare Beach. The Zion Hill Track goes left up the hill beside the toilet, halfway down the Pohutukawa Glade Track to the beach.

TRACK NOTES

○ The track is unmarked but well formed and signposted.

○ It climbs steeply for 45 minutes to the summit of Mount Zion (272 m) before meeting a junction with the Zion Ridge Track. Bear right and continue for 45 minutes as the track descends (at times steeply) to Pararaha Valley.

○ You can then return to Karekare along the coast.

The steep cliffs of the Waitakeres border the sandspit formed around Whatipu.

POINTS OF INTEREST

○ The views of the coastline south of Karekare towards Whatipu and the Pararaha Valley are ample reward for the climb.

○ The return trip along the beach features a short tunnel and remnants of raised embankments from the days when logs were transported by tram down the coast to Whatipu and the Manukau Harbour.

○ There is a wetlands reserve at the back of the beach, and dogs are not allowed. Those with a sense of adventure will find caves hidden beneath old pohutukawa at the base of the steep cliffs behind the embankment.

○ The narrow cover with steep cliffs rising straight from the beach, just before the rocky headland and Karekare Beach, was the setting for Jane Campion's film *The Piano*.

○ As you pass the rocks just before Karekare Beach you can still see the huge metal spikes that held the trestle framework onto the rocks.

40 Whatipu–Gibbons Track

GRADE 4

TIME 6 hours return

ACCESS The road to Whatipu follows the north head of the Manukau Harbour out to Huia, and then by an unsealed road to Whatipu. The track begins from the carpark.

TRACK NOTES

○ Take the Gibbons Track that leads up the hill to the right of the carpark (this is clearly marked). This track follows the top of the cliffs all the way to the Pararaha Valley (note that there are no short cuts down the cliffs to the beach). The track descends through the picturesque Pararaha Valley to the beach at Pararaha Point, then follows the beach back to Whatipu.

○ This walk, although not especially difficult, can turn into a very long trudge back along the beach for the unfit. Come prepared for a mini-expedition. Don't be tempted to take a short cut through the swampy area in the middle. Despite what look like tracks, these trails will soon lead you into knee-high water and dense vegetation that is surprisingly difficult to get out of.

○ The sea in this area is particularly treacherous and great care should be taken when swimming. Paratutae Rock in the harbour entrance looks very easy to climb but is extremely difficult to get back down.

POINTS OF INTEREST

○ Standing on the northern shores of the entrance to the Manukau Harbour, it is hard to believe that Auckland is a mere 50 minutes away by car. Yet the wild nature of the area belies the fact that this area was extensively farmed and milled, and even the shoreline bears little resemblance to that of 100 years ago. The sand dunes and swamp area below the cliffs didn't exist 150 years ago and are a good indication of the changing landscape.

○ The area was extensively milled for timber in the second half of the nineteenth century, and a tram railway was built from Paratutae Rock just inside the harbour mouth all the way to Karekare Beach. Evidence of the railway includes cuttings, embankments, spikes in rocks, a tunnel and a rusty boiler.

○ There are two large sea-caves at the base of the cliffs to the right of the carpark that are worth a visit.

○ The views from the cliff track are extensive, especially to the south where Mount Karioi near Raglan is visible on a clear day.

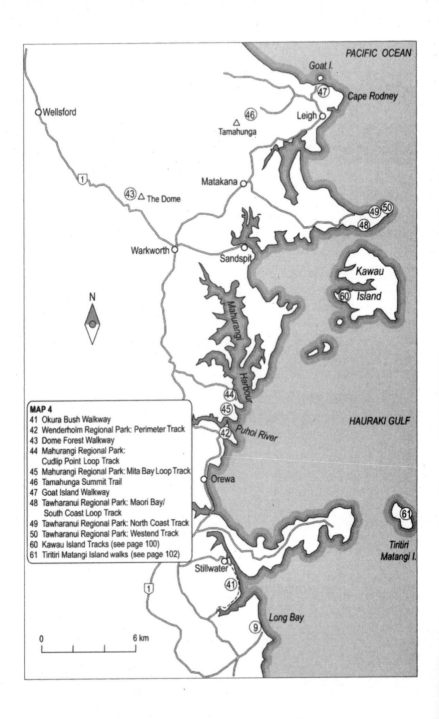

PACIFIC OCEAN

Goat I.

⑭47 Cape Rodney

Leigh

⑯46
Tamahunga

Wellsford

Matakana

43 △ The Dome

⑭49 ⑮50
⑭48

Warkworth

Sandspit

Kawau
Island

⑥60

Mahurangi

Harbour

HAURAKI GULF

⑭44
⑮45

⑭42 Puhoi River

Orewa

⑥61

Tiritiri
Matangi I.

N

MAP 4
41 Okura Bush Walkway
42 Wenderholm Regional Park: Perimeter Track
43 Dome Forest Walkway
44 Mahurangi Regional Park:
   Cudlip Point Loop Track
45 Mahurangi Regional Park: Mita Bay Loop Track
46 Tamahunga Summit Trail
47 Goat Island Walkway
48 Tawharanui Regional Park: Maori Bay/
   South Coast Loop Track
49 Tawharanui Regional Park: North Coast Track
50 Tawharanui Regional Park: Westend Track
60 Kawau Island Tracks (see page 100)
61 Tiritiri Matangi Island walks (see page 102)

Stillwater

⑭41

Long Bay

⑨9

0   6 km

NORTHERN WALKS

Hidden bays and sandy beaches feature strongly in the area north of Auckland City. Most of the walks are fairly short, but combined with a swim and views over the Hauraki Gulf, they make for a great day out. Two highly recommended walks are:

Okura Bush Walkway (4 hours return to Dacre Cottage)
This walk begins through an outstanding grove of puriri, then skirts the Okura River and ends up at historic Dacre Cottage combining the best of bush, sea and history.

Tawharanui Regional Park
A number of walks criss-cross the park, so you can make walking through this park as short or as long as you like. The walking is easy and open so you have unrestricted views out to Little Barrier Island and the Hauraki Gulf. Anchor Bay is one of the most beautiful beaches in the area and is ideal for swimming and surfing.

The scalloped coves of Anchor Bay are fringed by Tawharanui Regional Park.

41 Okura Bush Walkway

GRADE 3

TIME 2 hours one way to Dacre Cottage
3 hours one way to Stillwater

ACCESS Drive north for 4.5 km from the intersection of East Coast Bays Road and Oteha Valley Road, and turn left into Haigh Access Road. The track begins at the end of this road. The track description is from this starting point, but it can be accessed from Stillwater.

The Stillwater entrance is reached by driving a further 5.5 km north along East Coast Bays Road and turning right into Spur Road. Where the road divides, veer right into Duck Creek Road and then go to the very end, where the track starts by the Stillwater Motor Camp.

TRACK NOTES

○ The track begins at the carpark, crosses the Okura River on a bridge and enters the bush reserve, eventually coming out at the Okura River. To this point the track is well formed, but between the reserve and Dacre Point the track can be very boggy and muddy after periods of rain. However, unless the tide is very high you can walk along the sandy shore of the river as an alternative route all the way round to Dacre Cottage. For the short distance where the track crosses Dacre Point, the steep section can be slippery in wet weather.

The exposed rock shelf shows the extent of coastal erosion in the last 6500 years since the stabilisation of sea levels.

○ From Dacre Cottage the track continues north along the Weiti River to Stillwater.

POINTS OF INTEREST

○ Dacre Cottage is a lovingly restored and, unfortunately, frequently vandalised brick building nestled on the coastal flats at the fertile mouth of a river valley. It is situated back from the beach beside a chuckling creek.

○ Built by Ranulf Dacre in the 1850s, its interior is restored in the period of the day. Take time to read the 'Proclamation' on the door. Henry Dacre and his progeny farmed the area until 1963.

○ Pied oystercatchers and stilts fossick in the mudflats.

○ This coastline is a good example of the upper Waitemata area, exhibiting the rocks of the Waitemata Series, as well as sandy beaches, rocky platforms, shoreline mudflats and mangroves.

○ The coastal forest has some unusual tree specimens: an arching pohutukawa over the track, a nikau trunk which grows in a right angle, and the base of a kauri trunk that resembles the prow of a waka. A dense forest of nikau is regenerating beneath the canopy.

○ Of particular note is the beautiful grove of puriri trees in the reserve just after crossing the bridge.

○ The entire coastline is flanked by the Long Bay–Okura Marine Reserve, formed in 1995. The varied coastline harbours sandy shore communities at Karepiro Bay, intertidal zonation on the rocky reefs, and abundant food sources for fish and birds in the mudflats and mangroves near the Okura River.

42 Wenderholm Regional Park Perimeter Track

GRADE 3

TIME 1½ hours return

ACCESS From the parking area by Couldrey House, follow the wide metalled path to the west of the house. The start of the track is sign-posted up the hill to the left just after you pass through the Maori gateway. The track can also be accessed by a track on the north side of the Waiwera Bridge.

TRACK NOTES

○ For the first 30 minutes the track climbs through forest above coastal cliffs on a well-graded track, passing the Couldrey House Track junction on the right 100 m from the lookout. At this point you can return back to the carpark via the Couldrey House Track, which will take a further 30 minutes. If this is the option of choice it is worthwhile taking a short (20 m) detour to the lookout at the junction of the Couldrey House/Puhoi tracks.

○ After the lookout, the Perimeter Track drops into a shaded south-facing gully leading down to Kokopu Bay by the Waiwera River. This part of the track is steep and not as well formed as the other tracks in the park. Leaving Kokopu Bay the track continues uphill for about 30 minutes to the junction of the Puhoi and Perimeter tracks. The Perimeter Track runs along State Highway 1 north to the park entrance and access road. The constant drone of traffic on the highway can be off-putting on the last section and a better option is to turn right onto the Puhoi Track. This track climbs steeply through the bush to a wide grassed area and eventually joins up with the Couldrey House Track. Turn left onto this track and downhill back to the carpark.

POINTS OF INTEREST

○ In 1868 Robert Graham, the prominent Auckland politician and businessman who developed the nearby Waiwera bathhouse and hotel, bought some of the land and commissioned the building of the homestead. Many of the exotic trees in the grounds date from the time when Graham was the owner. He was friends with Sir George Grey, who owned nearby Kawau Island. Grey gifted many unusual specimens, including Caucasian fir, bunyabunya pine and Moreton Bay fig.

○ In 1944 the land was sold to the Couldrey family, who embarked on an extensive restoration of the dilapidated building.

○ In 1965, Wenderholm became Auckland's first regional park.

○ New Zealand pigeon, tui and fantail are common in the canopy of coastal forest, which contains magnificent groves of nikau as well as fine examples of puriri, kahikatea, kowhai, kanuka and taraire.

○ There are several excellent lookout points. On the eastern side of the reserve on the Perimeter Track a lookout gives wide views of the

Hauraki Gulf. The Puhoi Track has two lookouts, one a raised wooden platform looking south over the Waiwera River, and further up the hill near the junction of the Couldrey House Track the view is over the Puhoi River and to the north. Part way down the Couldrey House Track the view is over the Puhoi River, the beach and to the north.

○ At Kokopu Bay is an extensive grassed area suitable for picnics.

○ The pohutukawa lining the beachfront give a splendid display in the summer, and the kowhai flowers on the headland bloom in early spring.

○ If you are lucky, you might spot a banded rail or a fernbird in the wetlands at the mouth of the Puhoi River.

43 Dome Forest Walkway

GRADE 3

TIME 1 hour return

ACCESS The walkway is signposted from by the café at the top of Dome Hill, 6 km from Warkworth on State Highway 1 to Wellsford.

TRACK NOTES

○ The track steps steadily through native forest to a ridge on a metalled surface. The track along the ridge is well formed but uneven and latticed with tree roots.

POINTS OF INTEREST

○ The Dome Lookout faces southeast and looks to Warkworth and the eastern jaw of Mahurangi Harbour. The Dome Forest consists of 401 hectares of regenerating podocarp and broadleaf trees, which were logged in the early 1900s.

○ A canopy of kauri, rimu, miro, totara, kahikatea, taraire, puriri and kohekohe overtop an understorey of mapou, ponga, rangiora and mingimingi.

○ The tiny native Hochstetter's frog (*Leiopelma hochstetteri*) hides in damp places in the forest. The endemic species is very rare and misses out the tadpole stage in reproduction.

○ The Dome is said to be the final resting place of the Tainui ancestor Reipae and her sister Reitu. They are said to have flown to Whangarei Harbour on the back of a bird.

Mahurangi Regional Park (walks 44 and 45)

44 Cudlip Point Loop Track

GRADE 2

TIME 1½ hours return

ACCESS Mahurangi Regional Park is signposted off State Highway 1 along Mahurangi West Road. After 7 km, bear right into Ngarewa Drive and follow it to a parking area by Sullivans Bay. The start of the track is signposted up the headland at the southern end of the carpark.

TRACK NOTES

- The track is lined with red banded marker posts. After climbing steeply, the track crosses farm paddocks for 30 minutes to a 10-minute detour to the lookout at Cudlip Point.

- It then drops for 30 minutes to Te Muri Estuary, which can be crossed only at low tide. A walk along Te Muri Beach, dominated by a solitary, massive pohutukawa in its centre, will take approximately 30 minutes.

- The 15-minute return to the carpark is mostly along a metalled farm track.

- There are toilets and a campground at Sullivans Bay.

45 Mita Bay Loop Track

GRADE 3

TIME 1½ hours return

ACCESS From the carpark at Otarawao (Sullivans Bay), follow the signpost at the northern end of the beach.

TRACK NOTES

- The track is lined with blue banded marker posts and climbs steeply up and over a ridge through pasture for 30 minutes following the fenceline. After 25 minutes there is a lookout at Tungutu Point.

- After a further 15 minutes through Mita Bay, climb up the steep metalled farm track to Ngarewa Drive, from where it is 20 minutes along the entrance road to Sullivans Bay.

- There is an alternative route from Mita Bay to Sullivans Bay around the coastal rocks, which takes 20 minutes and is only possible at low tide.

POINTS OF INTEREST

○ Most of the rocks around Mahurangi were deposited as layers of sand and silt on the sea floor 20–25 million years ago. Uplift by the earth's tectonic forces has exposed the alternating strata and the cliffs are now eroded by wind, wave and water.

○ Before the close of the last Ice Age around 6500 years ago, sea levels rose by over 120 m, drowning river valleys such as Mahurangi to form harbours. From Tungutu Point on the Mita Bay Loop Track there are views up the harbour which bring this geological history to life.

○ These sheltered watercourses have since filled with mud and sand and been colonised by mangroves.

○ The relentless chipping away of the cliffs has exposed layers of rock at their base, which are now inhabited by intertidal marine creatures including snails, barnacles, mussels and crabs.

○ The abundance of shellfish on the rocky and sandy shores, the fishing in the calm estuarine water of Mahurangi Harbour, the plentiful eels and birds of the wetland and bush, and the ability to cultivate kumara made Mahurangi an attractive site for Maori occupation. Pa were constructed on headlands including Cudlip Point.

○ The earliest inhabitants were the Kawerau iwi of the Ngaoho people. In later times Ngati Paoa occupied the land and coast.

○ Sullivans Bay is named after John and Merihi Sullivan, whose descendants cleared and farmed the land. Otarawao means 'last place of refuge'.

46 Tamahunga Summit Trail

GRADE 3

TIME 3 hours return

ACCESS From Leigh, follow Pakiri Road to the top of Pakiri Hill and turn left into Rodney Road. The metalled road follows the ridge to a parking area at the roadend. The start of the track is signposted 200 m further on.

TRACK NOTES

○ For the first 45 minutes the track follows a fenceline over sometimes muddy and steep farmland. White bands are painted on the fenceposts.

○ Where the track enters the forest, it becomes less well formed but is clearly marked with orange triangles. After 45 minutes, it becomes steep and involves climbing over rocks for the final 15 minutes to the summit.

POINTS OF INTEREST

○ Tamahunga (436 m) is the highest point for a considerable distance in all directions. The coastal and landward views are best from the farmland section of the walk or from a lookout 5 minutes before reaching the summit trig.

○ The trail linked Ngati Wai territories in the north with Ngati Whatua tribal areas in the south. It was used by Te Kiri, a Ngati Wai chief who 'liberated' Maori war prisoners from Kawau Island in the 1860s.

○ Te Hiko o te Kiri (Tamahunga Summit Trail), which forms part of Te Araroa (the Long Pathway), was opened on 16 December 2001 by Sir Edmund Hillary. The wooden slab at the start of the walk was carved by Neil Devantier as part of Te Araroa celebrations.

47 Goat Island Walkway

GRADE 2

TIME $1\frac{1}{4}$ hours return

ACCESS From Leigh, Goat Island Marine Reserve is signposted along Pakiri Road. Turn right into Goat Island Road and follow it 1.5 km to the parking area on the left near the roadend.

The start of the track is signposted over the bridge at the bottom of the hill, on the right of the Auckland University Marine Laboratory buildings.

TRACK NOTES

○ The track is poorly marked but well formed. It crosses sometimes muddy paddocks for 20 minutes before entering regenerating coastal forest. It follows the cliff edge to the east of Goat Island.

○ The track peters out so you must return by the same route.

POINTS OF INTEREST

○ The area around Goat Island (Motu Hawere) is of special significance to Ngati Wai, as a treasured place for food-gathering.

○ In 1975 the Cape Rodney–Okakari Point Marine Reserve was established to protect the marine life in the area. The Auckland University Marine Laboratory complex nearby has studied how the populations of a wide variety of marine species have recovered since this protection was put in place. Goat Island is a 9-hectare rounded knoll with a fault line separating 180-million-year-old greywacke on the exposed seaward side and 10–15-million-year-old Waitemata Series rocks on the landward side.

○ The water here is excellent for swimming and snorkelling.

Tawharanui Regional Park (walks 48, 49 and 50)

Tawharanui Regional Park sits on the tip of a protruding limb of resistant greywacke (compacted layers of sanstone and silt, over 150 million years), which commands spectacular views in all directions.

Compared to the relative intimacy of inner Waitemata Harbour inlets and coves, the views at Tawharanui Regional Park are on a grander scale. The inner Hauraki Gulf islands are replaced with the Moehau Range of the Coromandel Peninsula, Great Barrier Island, Little Barrier Island, Hen and Chickens Islands and Bream Head.

Access to Tawharanui Regional Park is signposted past Matakana along Tokatu Road.

There are toilets at Anchor Bay and near the information buildings. Picnic tables and parking are at the lagoon carpark on the entrance road and at Anchor Bay at the roadend.

A network of tracks criss-cross the park. Most are either on a metalled surface or grass tracks over pastureland. There are three loop walks through pasture and forest, over craggy coastal rocks and along golden sandy beaches. A predator-proof fence now protects the park, making it a safe haven for birdlife.

Take care familiarising yourself with the track layout on the information panels, as it can be complicated to decipher.

The greywacke cliffs near Tokatu Point.

48 Maori Bay Coast Walk/South Coast Loop Track

GRADE 3

TIME $2\frac{1}{4}$ hours return

ACCESS The start of the track is signposted from the lagoon carpark.

TRACK NOTES

○ Three hours either side of low tide you can follow the coast from Jones Bay to Maori Bay. This takes 1 hour of hopping over coastal boulders, rock shelves and pebble-strewn beaches.

○ After approximately 45 minutes look for the large rock that resembles an unfurling elephant trunk. The steep grass track from Maori Bay is just the other side of the next headland.

○ The final part of the walk weaves for $1\frac{1}{4}$ hours through regenerating forest and pastureland along the South Coast Track. This section of the walk is signposted and marked with white banded posts.

POINTS OF INTEREST

○ The rockpools on the coastal section of the walk are interesting to dredge through.

○ Views are of the northern side of Kawau Island and the Kawau Channel, the sinuous coastline around Snells Beach and the eastern arm of Mahurangi Harbour.

49 North Coast Track

GRADE 3

TIME $3\frac{1}{2}$ hours return (including $1\frac{1}{2}$ hours return to Tokatu Point)

ACCESS The start of the track is signposted from Anchor Bay carpark.

TRACK NOTES

○ Follow the metalled coast road for 10 minutes and cross the footbridge. The start of the North Coast Track is signposted. This undulates over farmland for 45 minutes past a trig to the junction with the Tokatu Point Track.

○ You can spend $1\frac{1}{2}$ hours exploring the headland via Tokatu Loop Track or just 30 minutes walking to the magnificent lookout at Tokatu Point.

- An alternative return route via the Fisherman's Track is marked with red banded posts and cuts through forest. The track is partially metalled.

- You can also turn right and return along the Ecology Trail, marked with yellow banded posts, which provides the best walking surface.

- All return routes lead to Anchor Bay and take approximately 1¼ hours.

POINTS OF INTEREST

- At Tokatu Point, rare prostrate manuka forms low clumps. It usually grows as a tree, but in these exposed conditions remains low to the ground like a shrub.

- There are magnificent views of the outer Hauraki Gulf islands, which sit like sombre hulks on the horizon.

50 Westend Track

GRADE 2

TIME 1½ hours return

ACCESS The start of the track is signposted to the west of Anchor Bay carpark.

TRACK NOTES

- The track leads inland over pasture for 15 minutes along a low undulating ridge before bearing left through a cattleyard along a metalled farm track.

- The undulating climb over sometimes muddy pasture to the Pohutukawa Lookout takes 30 minutes. The track then drops to the beach (15 minutes).

- An alternative Shortcut Track is signposted from just after the cattle-yard. This cuts 15 minutes and the steeper gradient out of the journey to the western end of Anchor Bay.

- Follow the beach around Comet Rocks and Flat Rocks to return to Anchor Bay carpark (30 minutes).

POINTS OF INTEREST

- Little Barrier Island dominates the horizon like a monolith.

- The beaches are all north-facing and ideal for surfing, swimming and picknicking. A sprinkling of shells decorate the firm fine golden sand and dunefields recede behind.

The elevated viewing platform at the summit of Mount Auckland allows endless views in all directions.

○ A marine reserve stretches from Comet Rock to Tokatu Point on the north side of the park.

51 Mount Auckland Walkway

GRADE 3

TIME 2¾ hours return

ACCESS Mount Auckland Walkway is along Kaipara Hills Road, 26 km south of Wellsford along State Highway 16. Follow the unsealed road 3 km to a large parking bay on the right, from where the start of the walk is signposted.

TRACK NOTES

○ The track traverses farmland for 25 minutes. Bear left at the top of the farm track and follow the ridge over a low saddle before entering native forest in the Atuanui Conservation Area.

○ The track is then marked with orange triangles and is well formed with occasional muddy spots. The 1 hour to the summit passes two signposted detours to kauri trees (both less than 5 minutes return). The climb is gentle but steady and reaches a lookout platform by a trig on the 305 m summit.

○ The track across farmland is closed for lambing from 1 August to 30 September.

POINTS OF INTEREST

○ The best views of Kaipara Harbour are reserved for gaps in the vegetation before the summit. On a clear day there are extensive views from the elevated platform on the summit, which overtops the vegetation. You can see Bream Head, Hen and Chickens Islands, Little Barrier and Great Barrier islands, the Moehau Range of the Coromandel and everything in between.

○ The defensive ditch and middens near the summit indicate the presence of an earlier Maori pa site.

ISLANDS

The Hauraki Gulf contains over 40 islands, the smallest being little more than rocky outcrops through to the largest, Great Barrier, which guards the outer gulf. Favoured by both Maori and European settlers and easily accessible by sea, most of the islands have been highly modified, mainly by farming and logging.

All the islands retain an individuality, from historic Kawau to the volcanic landscape of Rangitoto, through to the world-renowned bird sanctuary of Tiritiri Matangi Island. Great Barrier Island has the most extensive bush areas and, having neither goats nor possums, retains much of its original flora and fauna.

The best-known islands are serviced by regular ferries and for most trips you will need to allow the best part of a day.

Highly recommended are:

Rangitoto Island (allow at least half a day)
Just 30 minutes from downtown Auckland, Rangitoto is Auckland's youngest island at a mere 600 years old. A combination of superb views, unique volcanic landscape and unusual plant life makes this trip hard to beat.

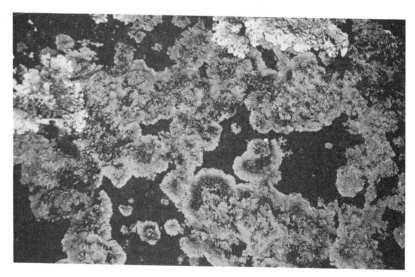

Lichen on scoria, Rangitoto Island.

Vegetation on scoria, Rangitoto Island.

Tiritiri Matangi Island (allow a full day)
Visting this island gives an opportunity to see some of this country's rarest birds such as saddleback and takahe. Tiritiri Matangi has been replanted by thousands of volunteers over the past 30 years. Good walking tracks, a historic lighthouse and gulf views make for a satisfying day out.

Kawau Island (allow a full day)
Although the walks are no longer than two hours, the historic Mansion House and the derelict copper mines make this an island well worth visiting.

Great Barrier Island (walks 52–58)

Great Barrier Island is the largest island off the North Island coast and the outermost island of the Hauraki Gulf. It is approximately 40 km long and 15 km wide, with a total area of 285 square kilometres. The east coast is open to the Pacific Ocean and has pristine beaches such as Medlands Beach, and large areas of dunes, swamps and mangroves. The west coast is more sinuous and rocky, with forested hills reaching to an idyllic coastline of coves, bays and inlets.

The central portion of the island is essentially volcanic in origin. Eruptions started 16–18 million years ago and continued with the formation of the 'West Barrier Volcano', which was probably centred offshore to the west of the present island. Erosive forces and weathering agents have since chiselled and sculpted the exposed rocks to form the spectacular landscape seen today. Walks such as Palmers Track through Windy Canyon to the top of Hirakimata/Mount Hobson give a dramatic impression of the scenery.

Windy Canyon, Great Barrier Island.

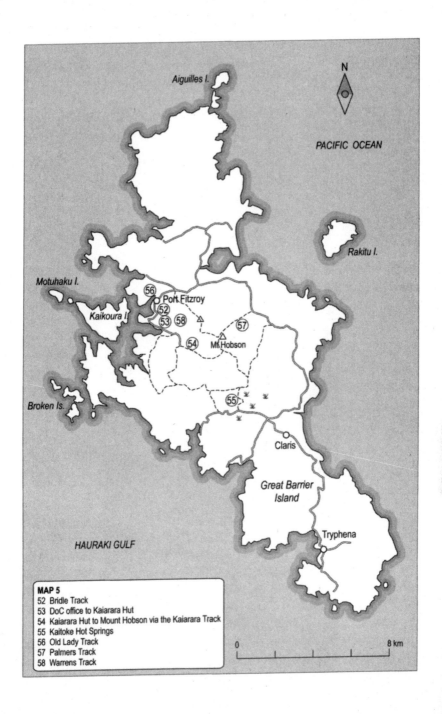

N

PACIFIC OCEAN

Aiguilles I.

Rakitu I.

Motuhaku I.

Kaikoura I.

56 Port Fitzroy
52
53 58
54 Mt Hobson
57

Broken Is.

55

Claris

Great Barrier
Island

HAURAKI GULF

Tryphena

MAP 5
52 Bridle Track
53 DoC office to Kaiarara Hut
54 Kaiarara Hut to Mount Hobson via the Kaiarara Track
55 Kaitoke Hot Springs
56 Old Lady Track
57 Palmers Track
58 Warrens Track

0   8 km

With the onset and waning of ice ages over the last 2 million years, sea levels have fluctuated. It is thought the Colville Channel, which separates Great Barrier Island from the Coromandel Peninsula, has been in existence for 10,000 years.

Since human colonisation, many of the predators that have wrought devastation on the mainland have thankfully been absent from Great Barrier Island. The forests remain free of possums, stoats, ferrets, weasels, deer, Norway rats and hedgehogs. Feral cats, deer, pigs and rats have had some impact, but the forest is notably more tuneful than its mainland counterpart. Birdlife in some areas is relatively prolific and endangered species such as the brown teal and the black petrel still breed on the island.

Brown teal.

The forest is composed of four main types, which vary according to altitude. Coastal forest merges with lowland mixed broadleaf forest. Lowland montane forest of kauri, rimu and towai occurs mostly between 250 m and 340 m above sea level, while the forest culminating at the summit of Mount Hobson (621 m above sea level) has a subalpine feel.

The Maori name Aotea means 'white cloud'. From around the thirteenth century, following the visit of the *Aotea* canoe, the Tutumaiao, Maewao or Turehu people inhabited the island. Ngati Rehua regard themselves as tangata whenua of the area. The island has been witness to many skirmishes due to its mild climate, fertile soils and proximity to abundant marine food resources.

Great Barrier Island's European name was given by Captain Cook, who recognised that the landmass sheltered the waters of the Hauraki Gulf. In the late 1700s and early 1800s, whaling ships started to pass by and following the discovery of copper in 1841, the first mining operation in New Zealand was established. Silver mining later took place and a battery was constructed at Oreville.

The kauri logging industry commenced in 1862, but only small blocks were felled until 1888, when large tracts of forest were purchased by the Kauri Timber Company. Felling subsequently began in earnest and, as exports from the island were not subject to customs duty before the First World War, a huge mill was established at Whangaparapara.

Kauri was rafted from the mainland and processed in what was reputed to be the largest mill in the southern hemisphere. A tramline was constructed, which crossed the island and transported logs from the east coast to Whangaparapara. Milling and felling continued until 1942, by which time 55 million feet of timber had been extracted. The Kaiarara Track passes some well-preserved remains of kauri dams on its way to the summit of Mount Hobson.

Various ferry companies operate regular services from Auckland to Great Barrier Island (for details, contact Auckland information centres). Some of these are vehicular ferries; however, there are taxi services and car rental companies on the island. Hitchhiking is possible around the island, although traffic flows, especially in the northern areas, can be very subdued.

Sixty percent of the island is administered by the Department of Conservation (DoC), which also runs several back-to-nature campsites. Contact the Great Barrier Island Area Office for up-to-date details on facilities and track conditions.

52 Bridle Track

GRADE 2

TIME 15 minutes one way

ACCESS The track is signposted from Port Fitzroy library, opposite Port Fitzroy store.

TRACK NOTES
○ The wide, even track climbs steadily through pine forest to level out through native forest. It then descends to the junction with Warren's Track just above Aotea Road, near the DoC office.

POINTS OF INTEREST
○ The walk provides a scenic short cut, although steeper, from Port Fitzroy wharf and store to the campground and DoC office at Akapoua.

53 DoC Office to Kaiarara Hut

GRADE 3

TIME 1 hour one way

ACCESS The DoC office is 20 minutes along the road from Port Fitzroy, passing the junction with the campsite and Bridle Track after 15 minutes.

TRACK NOTES

O From the DoC office, continue along the unsealed Kaiarara Bay Road over the headland for 30 minutes to the start of the Forest Road.

O After 5 minutes is a signposted detour (10 minutes return) to Blairs Landing. This narrow, partially overgrown track has no signpost at the shore end, but could be used as a starting point for people who have rowed ashore from a boat.

O From the detour, it is 20 minutes and two stream crossings to the junction with the Kiwiriki Track, and a further 5 minutes and one stream crossing (wet feet usually unavoidable) to Kaiarara Hut.

O Kaiarara Hut was renovated in 2002 and contains bunk space for 24 people. It has a cooking area with woodburner and cold rainwater supply.

POINTS OF INTEREST

O The views to the forested western isles and clear waters of Port Fitzroy harbour are glimpsed through the forest cover before reaching the Forest Road.

54 Kaiarara Hut to Mount Hobson via the Kaiarara Track

GRADE 4

TIME 3 hours one way

ACCESS The DoC office is 20 minutes along the road from Port Fitzroy, passing the junction with the campsite and Bridle Track after 15 minutes.

TRACK NOTES

O Cross the Kaiarara Stream twice (wet feet are usually unavoidable) and after 10 minutes pass the junction with the link to the South Fork Track. From here, it is a further 1 hour and three more stream crossings, on a sometimes uneven track, to the junction with Coopers Castle Route.

O After 15 minutes and two more stream crossings, a 5-minute return side-track leads to the well-preserved remains of the lower kauri dam.

Below Mount Hobson, Great Barrier Island.

○ A 1-hour climb leads to the upper dam at the top of the watershed. From here, it is 30 minutes to the summit of Mount Hobson. This final section of the track is on a boardwalk, with hundreds of steps, to protect the nesting sites of the black petrel. Please keep to the track.

POINTS OF INTEREST

○ Around 8–9 million years ago, a series of large eruptions in the Mount Hobson area contributed to the development of a large volcanic cone, which has since been eroded and weathered to form the spectacular series of bluffs, pinnacles and valleys seen today. Mount Hobson is at the hub of a series of spokes, which radiate in raised edges and give the area its dramatic landscape.

○ Mount Hobson/Hirakimata is 621 m above sea level. From the summit lookout platform, there are views of the entire island and north to the Hen and Chickens Islands, south to the Coromandel Peninsula and west to the greater Auckland region. The acidic volcanic rocks at the summit and high rainfall contribute to a montane forest, dominated by yellow-silver pine.

○ A remnant kauri forest still exists higher up the slopes, but most of it was logged from 1862 until 1940. When the Kauri Timber Company purchased the land containing the inaccessible stands of mature kauri

Lower dam, Great Barrier Island.

190

on the upper slopes of Mount Hobson, they used timber jacks and bullock teams to move the huge trunks into the streambeds.

○ Dams were built and 'tripped' during times of flood to release huge torrents of water, which collected the waiting logs. The upper dam was designed to hold a head of water, but the lower dam was constructed to allow logs to pass through. This type of dam was known as a stringer, as the planks were attached to the main structure by wires to stop them being carried downstream in a drive.

○ The 1926 stringer dam built by George Murray is 9.45 m wide and 4.27 m high. The dam was released by pulling a wire, which displaced a trigger and released a 'tom'. The structure is remarkably well pre-served and allows for easy viewing and exploration.

55 Kaitoke Hot Springs

GRADE 2

TIME 2 hours return

ACCESS The start of the walk is signposted from Whangaparapara Road, approximately 5 km before Whangaparapara.

TRACK NOTES
○ The track is wide and even. After 5 minutes it crosses a shallow stream, then undulates gently to the fork in the river by the hot springs.

POINTS OF INTEREST
○ The Kaitoke Hot Springs are a pool of hot water in a fork of the Kaitoke Stream. Maori often used the springs, but Europeans first frequented the steaming pools in the 1860s.

○ The water can reach 84°C, but is usually a more agreeable tem-perature. A concealed fault-line in the region allows deep-circulating groundwater to rise through the overlying rock and re-emerge in the forested enclave.

○ Industrious locals have constructed a ring of river rocks around one pool, beneath the languid fronds of overhanging ferns. The silted bottom provides a comfortable base, and well-placed rocks form 'pillows'. To avoid the danger of contracting amoebic meningitis, keep your head above water.

○ A picnic table is situated nearby.

56 Old Lady Track

GRADE 2; 3 to Lookout Rock

TIME 1½ hours return; 2 hours return including detour to Lookout Rock

ACCESS From the wharf at Port Fitzroy, continue past the store (5 minutes) to Glen Fern Road (on the left). The start of the track is signposted on the right.

TRACK NOTES

○ The track is wide and even as it climbs a forested gully to the summit of Aotea Road and the turnoff to Karaka Bay. Five minutes after the initial shallow stream crossing is a signposted detour to Lookout Rock. After 20 minutes of steady climbing, the track forks; right is 5 minutes to the summit of Lookout Rock, left is a 10-minute steeper descent to rejoin the Old Lady Track, 10 minutes above the lower junction.

○ From here, it is a further 25 minutes to the end of the main track.

○ Return by the same track or follow the unsealed Aotea Road.

POINTS OF INTEREST

○ The verdant coastal forest of nikau, puriri and kohekohe is alive with the calls of tui and bellbirds and the flap of New Zealand pigeon wings.

Looking towards Port Fitzroy, Great Barrier Island.

○ The views from Lookout Rock over Port Fitzroy Harbour show the winding forested coastline with its calm blue waters reflecting the sunlight. Occasional buildings sit in grassed clearings and sailing boats are anchored in the secluded coves.

57 Palmers Track

GRADE 2 to Windy Canyon; 4 to Hirakimata/Mount Hobson

TIME 30 minutes return to Windy Canyon
    4 hours return to Mount Hobson

ACCESS The start of the track is signposted from the summit of Whanga-poua Hill on Aotea Road between Awana and Okiwi.

TRACK NOTES

○ After 10 minutes the well-formed and even track reaches the steps through the intimate gorges of Windy Canyon.

○ After a further 30 minutes through the gorges over a narrow, well formed and undulating track, you reach a 'wooden horse', a relic from the logging days.

○ For the final $1\frac{1}{4}$ hours to the summit, the track is very steep, narrow and uneven.

○ The boardwalk over the final stages below the summit is there to protect the nesting sites of the endangered black petrel. Please keep to the track.

POINTS OF INTEREST

○ Around Windy Canyon, the stepped track passes through the close vegetation and encrusted walls of volcanic obsidian. The pinnacles, jagged bluffs and convoluted outcrops protrude through the forest, creating an otherworldliness to the landscape.

○ The volcanic rocks have steadily been reworked along weaknesses and fractures by rain and running water to produce the narrow ravines around Windy Canyon. The heathland in the area contains Great Barrier tea-tree (*Kunzea sinclairii*) and the daisy shrub (*Olearia allomii*), both unique to Great Barrier Island.

○ The 'wooden horse' is also known as a snatch box and once housed a double pulley. This arrangement was powered by a steam hauler to drag logs from the Awana Stream over the ridge to the waiting bullock teams, which pulled the logs to Whangaparapara Harbour.

○ Mount Hobson is 621 m above sea level. From the summit lookout platform there are views of the entire island and north to the Hen and Chickens Islands, south to the Coromandel Peninsula and west to the Greater Auckland region. The acid volcanic rocks at the summit and high rainfall contribute to a montane forest, dominated by yellow-silver pine.

○ The black petrels breed only on Great Barrier and Little Barrier islands. Their total population is estimated to be 3000–4000 birds, and over 800 pairs are thought to breed on Mount Hobson. They breed in late spring, lay one egg in a burrow, and the young leave the nests between April and July.

58 Warrens Track

GRADE 2

TIME 50 minutes return

ACCESS The start of the track is signposted opposite the DoC office at Akapoua, 1 km south of Port Fitzroy.

TRACK NOTES

○ The track is wide and even for 20 minutes, crossing the shallow stream twice before following it 20 m along its rocky bank to a waterfall.

○ For 25 minutes to the junction with the Bridle Track (5 minutes from the DoC office), the track is wide, metalled and even.

POINTS OF INTEREST

○ The series of swimming holes culminate in a small waterfall cascading gently through the shaded gully.

Rangitoto Island

59 Rangitoto Island Summit Track

GRADE 2

TIME 2–3 hours

ACCESS Ferries to Rangitoto leave from the wharf by the Ferry Building at the bottom of Queen Street. The ferry trip takes around 30 minutes. For information contact Fullers, (09) 367 9111, www.fullers.co.nz.

Rangitoto Island.

TRACK NOTES

○ The summit track from the wharf is well formed, well marked and is a steady climb, though a little steep near the top. You can return to the wharf via Islington Bay to the east or McKenzie Bay to the west, but these alternatives are lengthy trips and you will need to walk briskly in order to catch the return ferry.

○ Carry plenty of water, as walking on the island can be very hot and dry (water is available at the facilities at the wharf). If you want to explore the caves, bring a torch.

POINTS OF INTEREST

○ Iconic Rangitoto is one of Auckland's best walks. The view from the summit (260 m) is superb and takes in the Hauraki Gulf and Auckland city and surrounds.

○ Rangitoto was still active less than 400 years ago, and is less than 600 years old. The most recent lava flows are on the west side below the summit. The name means 'blood sky', which, though very appropriate, is thought to refer to wounds suffered by a Maori chief on the island.

○ A short side-track leading off to the right just below the summit takes you to a series of lava caves large enough to walk through. These are best explored with a torch.

○ The vegetation is surprisingly varied — lush bush near the summit contrasts with the toughest of plants, barely surviving in the harsh environment of the lava fields. Of special interest are the kidney ferns, which are lush and moist when wet, only to shrivel away to a dry papery texture in order to survive the hot weather.

○ Short walks from the wharf area are worth investigating. Colonies of nesting seabirds are common in the summer, and along the shoreline are penguin nesting boxes, which allow the visitor to see the penguins without disturbing them.

○ Swimming is possible at high tide around the wharf area.

Kidney fern, Rangitoto Island.

○ A feature of Rangitoto Island is the old baches (beach cottages), which date from the first half of last century. There is now a movement to preserve the remaining baches.

○ Many of the roads, paths and stone walls were built by prisoners in the 1920s and 1930s.

Bach, Rangitoto Island.

Kawau Island

60 Kawau Island Tracks

GRADE 2

TIME 2 hours return

ACCESS Two ferries travel to the island: 360 Discovery, 0800 360 3472, and Kawau Water Taxis, 0800 111 616.

TRACK NOTES

○ All tracks on Kawau Island pass under a canopy of radiata pines, with a carpet of needles on the forest floor. The tracks are well formed and signposted, but mostly unmetalled.

○ From the wharf at Mansion House Bay follow the front fence of Mansion House to the right and climb the headland to Momona Point. The track loops back and follows cliffs along the western coastline to Lady's Bay (30 minutes). After 15 minutes, at the grass clearing and lookout, follow the Miners Track for 15 minutes to the old copper mine. At low tide, walk across the rocks to the ruins of the copper mine engine house.

○ Past the chimney the track climbs to a grass clearing from where the Redwood Track leads through a shady gully to Two House Bay (45 minutes).

○ The 15-minute climb back over the steep headland to Mansion House Bay is metalled.

POINTS OF INTEREST

○ Ngati Tai lived on the island, fiercely guarding the nearby renowned fishing grounds containing bountiful muru (small spotted shark). They cultivated land around Momona Point (momona means 'fertile land').

○ In the 1830s green stains were noticed on the cliffs near South Cove and this prompted the exploration for copper and manganese. In 1844 both were discovered and mined, in one of New Zealand's earliest industries. Over 3000 tonnes of copper were removed, with a value of £60,000. Mining ceased in 1855, but the 70-foot-high brick chimney of the engine house still stands at Dispute Cove.

○ In 1862 Sir George Grey bought Kawau Island for £3500 and invested

This copper mine chimney is the most obvious industrial relic on Kawau Island.

his love of arts and natural history, energy, and a hint of eccentricity into creating a private kingdom. He planted exotic botanical species, brought from his time in Australia and South Africa. He introduced animals such as zebra, Chinese peacock, monkey, antelope, kookaburra and wallaby. Today the Parma wallabies, which became extinct in their native Australia, are a pest on the island, and many have been shipped home.

○ George Grey was premier of New Zealand between 1877 and 1879 and lived at Mansion House from 1870 until 1874. He collected 8000 rare books, which he gifted to Auckland Public Library, and was socially egalitarian, building a school for his employees' children at School House Bay. He sold Kawau Island in 1888 for £12,000 and died in 1898 with £800 to his name.

○ Today these remnants of the island's history form an exotic mix that adds a unique and warm atmosphere to a walk around the island. Although the walks can be accomplished in 2 hours, you are better to spend the day on the island and explore Mansion House as well.

Tiritiri Matangi Island

61 Tiritiri Matangi Island walks

GRADE 2

TIME There is a variety of short and longer walks on the island but as you are reliant on the ferry service, allow a full day.

ACCESS 360 Discovery run ferries from both downtown Auckland and Sandspit, 0800 360 3472, www.360discovery.co.nz.

TRACK NOTES

○ From the wharf a track leads up to the lighthouse (about 30 minutes) and from there a network of well-formed and clearly marked tracks spread out over the island. Although the island is not very large or particularly hilly, the track system is extensive, so plan your walk to suit your party. The longest walk will take 3–4 hours and there are some steep sections.

○ The East Coast Track begins behind the lighthouse and runs the length of the eastern side of the island with side-tracks to a number

Cabbage trees are only one of the many native species you can see on Tiritiri Matangi. Trees such as this have been planted as part of the huge flora and fauna restoration programme on the island.

of small bays. Several tracks run back up to the Ridge Track in case time or fitness is an issue. From the end of the East Coast Track, the Ngati Paoa Loop goes down to North East Bay which, although rocky, is a good place to swim. From the loop take the Ridge Track back to the Kawerau Track down to Hobbs Bay and the wharf.

○ The two key birdwatching areas are Wattle Track and Kawerau Track, and both have bird-feeding stations, so you are guaranteed to see birds. Wattle Track leads up from the wharf to the lighthouse. From there, take the Ridge Track for about 1 km, and Kawerau Track leads off to the left down to Hobbs Beach. Both tracks are well formed and include boardwalks and quiet seating areas.

POINTS OF INTEREST

○ You will be met at the wharf on the island by a local DoC ranger who will give you a brief introduction to the island's history. For a small fee you can take a guided walk from the ferry to the lighthouse via the Wattle Track. This is highly recommended and will significantly add to your appreciation of this unique island (the money helps fund projects on the island). A shop at the lighthouse sells gifts and books.

○ Tiritiri Matangi is an open bird sanctuary and for most people a visit to the island will be the only opportunity to see rare New Zealand birds such as takahe, brown teal, saddlebacks, kakariki and stitchbird. The feeding stations on the Kawerau and Wattle tracks are the best places to see bellbirds and stitchbirds, but it pays to sit in any part of the bush and quietly observe the birdlife. Kiwi and kokako are also on the island, but are more difficult to spot.

○ For more than 20 years volunteer groups have planted native trees and shrubs on this island, which was previously virtually stripped of native vegetation. The result is a haven for endangered birds. As most of the vegetation is still young, these birds are clearly visible above and in the low canopy. The birdsong is in direct contrast to the silent bush on the mainland.

○ North East Bay is a good stopping point for those doing the longer walk. It is suitable for swimming.

○ In the northwest part of the island are two historic pa sites.

○ Hobbs Bay, about 5 minutes' walk from the wharf, is the best swimming beach.

The lighthouse on Tiritiri Matangi Island.

○ The historic lighthouse began operating in 1865 and at one stage had the most powerful light in the southern hemisphere at 11 million candlepower.

Waiheke Island

62 Stoney Batter Walkway

GRADE 2

TIME 2 hours return

ACCESS While the walk from the end of the road to Stoney Batter is easy, getting there is the tricky part. Transport from the wharf varies from season to season so it is best to check with the Waiheke Island Visitor Information Centre, (09) 372 1234, before you set out (the centre also has a small booklet on other walks). For ferry information contact Fullers, (09) 367 9111, www.fullers.co.nz.

TRACK NOTES

○ The track begins off Man o' War Road about 6 km from Onetangi and is clearly marked across farmland.

○ A torch is essential.

POINTS OF INTEREST

○ The Second World War fortifications are the best preserved and the most extensive in the Auckland area and are well worth a visit. Although the large guns have gone nearly everything else is intact and accessible. Stairways, tunnels, living areas and the gun emplacements cover a wide area and in many places the concrete still looks freshly poured.

○ Stoney Batter takes its name from the unusual rocky outcrops formed 8 million years ago by volcanic activity.

○ A bonus are the extensive views out across the Hauraki Gulf.

A gun pit alongside the Stoney Batter Walkway, Waiheke Island.

63 Matiatia/Owhanake Loop

GRADE 2

TIME 3 hours

ACCESS The walk begins and ends at the Matiatia Wharf, but Oneroa is within easy walking distance for those wanting to take in a café or a swim at Oneroa Bay.

TRACK NOTES

○ The starting point is to the left of the wharf, and follows the shoreline via Matiatia Historic Reserve, Cable Bay and Owhaneke Bay. From Owhaneke Bay take the wide track at the southern end of the bay up to Delamore Road, then the track down through a reserve to Ocean View Road, which will lead back to the wharf.

POINTS OF INTEREST

○ Waiheke Island is the second largest island in the Gulf and, although it has very little in the way of bush, it does have beautiful beaches, cafés and vineyards.

○ The views back to the city and inner Gulf are superb and near Delamore Road are the traces of an ancient pa site as well as pillboxes built during the Second World War.